T0103321

HOW SUCCESSFUL
PEOPLE LEAD

Books by Dr. John C. Maxwell
Can Teach You How to Be a REAL Success

Relationships

25 Ways to Win with People

Becoming a Person of Influence

Encouragement Changes Everything

Ethics 101

Everyone Communicates, Few Connect

The Power of Partnership

Relationships 101

Winning with People

Attitude

Attitude 101

The Difference Maker

Failing Forward

How Successful People Think

Success 101

Thinking for a Change

The Winning Attitude

Equipping

The 15 Invaluable Laws of Growth

The 17 Essential Qualities of a Team Player

The 17 Indisputable Laws of Teamwork

Developing the Leaders Around You

Equipping 101

Make Today Count

Mentoring 101

My Dream Map

Partners in Prayer

Put Your Dream to the Test

Running with the Giants

Talent Is Never Enough

Today Matters

Your Road Map for Success

Leadership

The 10th Anniversary Edition of The 21 Irrefutable Laws of Leadership

The 21 Indispensable Qualities of a Leader

The 21 Most Powerful Minutes in a Leader's Day

The 360 Degree Leader

Developing the Leader within You

The 5 Levels of Leadership

Go for Gold

Leadership 101

Leadership Gold

Leadership Promises for Every Day

HOW
SUCCESSFUL
PEOPLE
LEAD

TAKING YOUR INFLUENCE
TO THE NEXT LEVEL

JOHN C. MAXWELL

**CENTER
STREET**

NEW YORK   BOSTON   NASHVILLE

The author is represented by Yates & Yates, LLP,

Literary Agency, Orange, California.

Originally Published as *The 5 Levels of Leadership* by Center Street, 2011.

Diagram of the 5 Levels of Leadership designed by Alex Watson

Scripture taken from the New King James Version (NKJV)

Copyright © 1982 by Thomas Nelson, Inc. Used by permission.

All rights reserved

Scripture taken from the New American Standard Bible® (NASB),

Copyright © 1960, 1962, 1963, 1968, 1971, 1972, 1973, 1975, 1977, 1995 by The Lockman Foundation. Used by permission.

Center Street
Hachette Book Group
1290 Avenue of the Americas
New York, NY 10104

www.CenterStreet.com

Printed in China

APS

First edition: May 2013
21

Center Street is a division of Hachette Book Group, Inc.
The Center Street name and logo are trademarks of Hachette Book Group, Inc.

The Hachette Speakers Bureau provides a wide range of authors for speaking events. To find out more, go to www.HachetteSpeakersBureau.com or call (866) 376-6591.

The publisher is not responsible for websites (or their content) that are not owned by the publisher.

Library of Congress Cataloging-in-Publication Data
Maxwell, John C., 1947–
  How successful people lead : taking your influence to the next level / John C. Maxwell.—First Edition.
    pages cm
  Includes index.
  ISBN 978-1-59995-362-5 (hbk.)—ISBN 978-1-4555-4545-2 (large print : hbk.)—ISBN 978-1-4555-7383-7 (ebk.) 1. Leadership. 2. Leadership—Social aspects. I. Title.
  HD57.7.M394258 2013
  658.4'092—dc23
                                                                    2012040800

This book is dedicated to EQUIP (www.iequip.org) and all the people who are a part of this leadership organization.

EQUIP's Rule of 5:

Every day we…

Think Globally

Evaluate Our Leadership Strategy

Create Resources

Develop Associate Trainers, Partners, and Donors

Train Leaders to Train Leaders

Millions of leaders are being trained
because of your efforts. Thanks!

Contents

Acknowledgments

Thank you to:

Charlie Wetzel, my writer;

Stephanie Wetzel, my social media manager;

Linda Eggers, my executive assistant.

Introduction

If your vision of success includes starting an organization, owning a company, or putting together a team, you need to become good at leadership. If you cannot lead well, you will not be successful.

When I discovered this, leadership became one of my passions. I love learning about it. I also enjoy teaching it. I've dedicated more than thirty years of my life to helping others learn what I know about leading. In fact, I spend about eighty days every year teaching leadership. In the last several years, I've taught it on six continents. The subject is inexhaustible. Why? Because everything rises and falls on leadership. If you want to make a positive impact on the world, learning to lead better will help you do it.

In all the years that I've taught leadership, there has been one lecture that I have been asked to give more often than any other—from West Point to Microsoft headquarters and in countries all around the world. Why is it so popular? That lecture explains how successful people lead and provides a game plan for learning how to become a leader. It's titled "The 5 Levels of Leadership," and it has been used to train leaders in companies of every size and configuration, from small businesses to Fortune 100 companies. It has been used to help nonprofit organizations understand how to lead volunteers. And taught in more than 120 countries around the world. The concept is tested and proven. It also instructs people in the use of several tried-and-true techniques that will help them become successful at leadership.

Looking at leadership as a series of levels that can be gained through targeted actions has many benefits. Here are just a few:

It Creates a Clear Picture of Leadership

For those who are not naturally gifted at it, leadership can be a mystery. For them, leading people is like walking down a dark corridor. They have a sense of where they want to go, but they can't see ahead and they don't know where the problems and pitfalls are going to lie. For many people in the academic world, leadership is a theoretical exercise, an equation whose variables are worthy of research, study, and rigorous debate. In contrast, the 5 Levels of Leadership is visually straightforward, so anyone can learn it.

It Defines *Leading* as a Verb, Not a Noun

Leadership is a process, not a position. There was a time when people used the terms *leadership* and *management* interchangeably. I think most people now recognize that there is a significant difference between the two. Management is at its best when things stay the same.

Leadership deals with people and their dynamics, which are continually changing. The challenge of leadership is to create change and facilitate growth. Those conditions require movement, which, as you will soon see, is inherent in moving up from one level of leadership to the next.

It Breaks Down Leading into Understandable Steps

The subject of leadership can be overwhelming and confusing. Where does leadership start? What should we do first? What processes should we use? How can we gain influence with others? How can we develop a productive team? How do we help followers become leaders in their own right? The 5 Levels of Leadership gives answers to these questions using understandable steps.

It Provides a Clear Game Plan for Leadership Development

Too often when people think of their journey into leadership, they envision a career path. What they should be thinking about is their own leadership development! Good leadership isn't about advancing yourself. It's about advancing your team. The 5 Levels of Leadership provides clear steps for leadership growth. Lead people well and help members of your team to become effective leaders, and a successful career path is almost guaranteed.

It Aligns Leadership Practices, Principles, and Values

When I developed the 5 Levels, I conceived of each level as a practice that could be used to lead more effectively. As time went by and I used and taught the levels, I realized they were actually principles. Here's the difference: a practice is an action that may work in one situation but not necessarily in another. A principle is an external truth that is as reliable as a physical law. For example, when Solomon said, "A gentle answer turns away wrath, but a harsh word stirs up anger," he stated a principle that is universal and timeless. Principles are important because they function as a map, allowing us to make wise decisions. If we embrace a principle and internalize it, it becomes a part of our values. The 5 Levels influences my leadership life every day.

How Leadership Works

How do people learn leadership? For most, it's through trial and error. While some things come only through experience, I believe the framework for how leadership works can be learned by looking at the 5 Levels. So let's start with an overview and a few insights about the Levels and how they work. Then we can look at each level individually in the subsequent sections of this book. As you look at each level, you will learn the upside, downside, and best behaviors for that level. You will also become acquainted with the beliefs that help a leader move up to the next level.

Level 1—Position
People follow you because they have to.

Position is the lowest level of leadership—the entry level. The only influence a positional leader has is that which comes with the job title. Positional leadership is based on the rights granted by the position and title. Nothing is wrong with having a leadership position. Everything is wrong with using position to get people to follow you. Position is a poor substitute for influence.

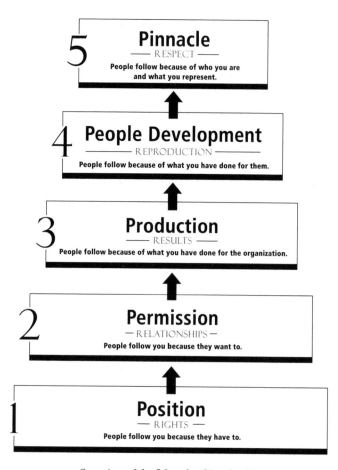

Overview of the 5 Levels of Leadership

People who make it only to Level 1 may be bosses, but they are never leaders. They have subordinates, not team members. They rely on rules, regulations, policies, and organization charts to control their people. Their people will only follow them within the stated boundaries of their authority. And their people will usually do only what is required of them. When positional leaders ask for extra effort or time, they rarely get it.

Positional leaders usually have difficulty working with volunteers, younger people, and the highly educated. Why? Because positional leaders have no influence, and these types of people tend to be more independent.

Position is the only level that does not require ability and effort to achieve. Anyone can be appointed to a position.

Level 2—Permission

People follow you because they want to.

Level 2 is based entirely on relationships. On the Permission level, people follow because they want to. When you like people and treat them as individuals who have value, you begin to develop influence with them. You develop trust. The environment becomes much more positive—whether at home, on the job, at play, or while volunteering.

The agenda for leaders on Level 2 isn't preserving their position. It's getting to know their people and figuring out how to get along with them. Leaders find out who their people are. Followers find out who their leaders are. People build solid, lasting relationships.

You can like people without leading them, but you cannot lead people well without liking them. That's what Level 2 is about.

Level 3—Production

People follow you because of what you have done for the organization.

One of the dangers of getting to the Permission level is that a leader may be tempted to stop there. But good leaders don't just create a pleasant working environment. They get things done! That's why they must move up to Level 3, which is based on results. On the Production level, leaders gain influence and credibility, and people begin to follow them because of what they have done for the organization.

Many positive things begin happening when leaders get to Level 3. Work gets done, morale improves, profits go up, turnover goes down, and goals are achieved. It is also on Level 3 that momentum kicks in.

Leading and influencing others becomes fun on this level. Success and productivity have been known to solve a lot of problems.

On Level 3, leaders can become change agents. They can tackle tough problems and face thorny issues. They can make the difficult decisions that will make a difference. They can take their people to another level of effectiveness.

Level 4—People Development

People follow you because of what you have done for them.

Leaders become great not because of their power but because of their ability to empower others. That is what leaders do on Level 4. They use their position, relationships, and productivity to invest in their followers and develop them until those followers become leaders in their own right. The result is reproduction; Level 4 leaders reproduce themselves.

Production may win games, but People Development wins championships. Two things always happen on Level 4. First, teamwork goes to a very high level because the high investment in people deepens relationships, helps people to know one another better, and strengthens loyalty. Second, performance increases because there are more leaders on the team, and they help to improve everybody's performance.

Level 4 leaders change the lives of the people they lead, and the people follow them because of that. Their relationships are often lifelong.

Level 5—Pinnacle

People follow you because of who you are
and what you represent.

The highest and most difficult level of leadership is the Pinnacle. While most people can learn to climb to Levels 1 through 4, Level 5 requires not only effort, skill, and intentionality but also a high level of talent. Only naturally gifted leaders ever make it to this highest level. Level 5 leaders develop people to become Level 4 leaders.

Developing leaders to the point where they are able and willing to develop other leaders is the most difficult leadership task of all. But here are the payoffs: Level 5 leaders develop Level 5 organizations. They create opportunities that other leaders don't. Their leadership gains a positive reputation. They create legacy in what they do. As a result, Level 5 leaders often transcend their position, their organization, and sometimes their industry.

Insights on Leading
from the Levels

If you want to become an effective leader and lead the way successful people do, then you must master the 5 Levels of Leadership. You must learn to recognize where you stand with each person in regard to the Levels, work to establish your credibility and gain influence where you are, and earn your way up to higher levels. If you learn this and live it day after day, you will be able to lead the way successful people do.

Now that you are acquainted with the Levels and how influence is gained on each, I want to share some insights that will help you to understand how the Levels relate to one another.

1. You Can Move Up a Level but You Never Leave the Previous One Behind

You may assume that a leader climbs the Levels, leaving one to arrive at the next, the way a person moves up a staircase. But the truth is that you never leave a level behind after you've achieved it. Instead, you simply build upon it. If you think about it for a moment, you'll agree that it makes sense.

If you start out with a leadership position and you build relationships with the people you oversee, do you resign your position to do so? No. You don't leave your position to advance, but if you win Level 2 correctly, you never need to rely on your position again.

Once you've built relationships with people and move to a higher level of productivity, do you abandon or neglect those relationships? You had better not! If you do, you'll find yourself back down at Level 1 again.

Leaders don't trade one level for another. They add a new level to the previous one. It is a building process.

2. You Are Not on the Same Level with Every Person

Leadership is dynamic, and it changes from relationship to relationship. The same is true for the 5 Levels of Leadership. I may be on a different one of the 5 Levels with each of five different people at my job. A person on his or her first day at work will acknowledge only my position, while someone in whom I've invested and whom I've raised up to lead will likely put me on Level 4. If I've been a good father at home, I may be on Level 4 with my children. If I've been an absentee dad, I may be on Level 1. With my next-door neighbor, perhaps I'm on Level 2. People will respond to you based on the level of leadership you've established with them. And that is subject to change.

Good leaders do not lead everyone the same way, because every person is different and you're not on the same level of leadership with every person. Effective leaders interact with followers based on:

- Where they are with each specific follower,
- Where the followers perceive the leader to be, and
- Where the followers are in their own leadership development.

Each of these factors comes into play as you evaluate your leadership and work to develop it.

Achieving a level of leadership is not like earning a degree. Nor is it like setting a performance record as an athlete. You don't achieve it and leave it. It's more like having to run a race every day to prove your ability. The lone exception is the Pinnacle. Leaders who rise to Level 5 are sometimes given credit for being on that level by virtue of their reputation, not just their personal interactions with followers. But it's important to note that at any level, a leader doesn't always automatically stay at that level. You must earn your level of leadership with each person, and that level can go up or down at any time.

3. The Higher You Go, the Easier It Is to Lead Others

Here's some good news. As you work to climb up the levels of leadership, you'll find that it gets easier to lead people. Each advance allows you to be more effective in leading others because your influence increases as you go to a higher level. As your influence increases, more people follow you more readily. Limited influence, limited leadership. Greater influence, greater effectiveness. That's common sense. However, there's also some bad news: it's not easy to climb the levels of leadership! If it were easy, everyone would be a Level 5 leader.

4. The Higher You Go, the More Time and Commitment Is Required to Win a Level

There is no easy way to get to the top. You have to be more committed, you have to give more, you have to use more energy, each time you want to go up a level. And so do your people. Nobody achieves anything great by giving the minimum. No teams win championships without making sacrifices and giving their best.

5. Moving Up Occurs Slowly, But Going Down Can Happen Quickly

Building always takes a lot longer than destroying. A lot of things have to be right before you can climb to a higher level, but sometimes it takes only one thing going wrong to cause someone to fall. For example, think about how long it takes to build a great relationship with a person. But if you do something to lose trust with that person, the relationship can become permanently broken in the blink of an eye.

While it's unsettling to think about how quickly one can fall from a level of leadership, I hope you can take solace in this: once you've climbed up to higher levels, the levels below you function as a safety net. So the more you've advanced up the levels, the more secure your leadership is. For example, if you make some bad decisions on Level 3 that ruin your productivity or that of the team, the relationships you've developed may save you from being fired. The only level without a safety net is the lowest one: Position. You don't get too many chances to make mistakes on that level. That's another good reason to work your way up the levels of leadership.

6. The Higher You Go, the Greater the Return

You may give more to climb to higher levels of leadership, but you get more, too. As a leader, you reap a greater return on your investment with each level you reach. On Level 2, you earn trust and the right to lead. On Level 3, you add to the productivity of the organization. On Level 4, you multiply that productivity because every time you add another leader to an organization, you add all the horsepower of that leader's team. On Level 5, the growth and productivity become exponential as you add leaders to the organization who not only lead others but also create generations of leaders who keep on producing.

The better the leaders are in an organization, the better everyone in the organization becomes. When productivity is high, chemistry is good, morale is high, and momentum is strong, then the payoffs increase.

7. Moving Farther Up Always Requires Further Growth

Each time a leader moves up to a higher level of leadership, greater skill is required. For that reason, each step of growth requires further development on the part of the leader. But that growth also functions as a platform from which a leader can grow into the next.

Here's how this works. To grow to a new level, leaders take risks. At the lower levels, the risks are smaller and more easily won. For example, to make the climb from Level 1 to Level 2, leaders risk initiating relationships. When leaders get to higher levels, the risks get bigger. For example, on Level 3, leaders may rally the team to try to accomplish a lofty goal, only to fail; that could cost the leader credibility, stop momentum, and demotivate team members. But here's the good news: Every risk at a higher level is a natural extension of the skills that leaders have by then developed. Outsiders might look at a leader and say, "Wow, he really stepped out and took a big risk." But those observers may not see the growth that has occurred in the leader. By the time the next risk must be undertaken, the leader has grown into it.

Growing as a leader requires a combination of intentional growth and leadership experience. If people rely only on experience without intentionally learning and preparing for the next level, they won't progress as leaders. On the other hand, if they only prepare mentally yet obtain no experience through risk and reward, and trial and error, then they still won't progress. It takes both—plus some amount of talent. But you have no control over how much talent you possess. You control only what you do with it.

If you possess a natural gift for leadership, you probably have a passion for growth. You like to see things build. It's part of your wiring. Go with it. If you have a more modest amount of talent, don't lose hope. You can make up for a lot by becoming a highly intentional student of leadership, thereby making the most of every opportunity. Either way, remember that success at any level helps you to be successful at every level. So work hard to win the level you're working toward now. It will prepare you for the future.

8. Not Climbing the Levels Limits You and Your People

The Law of the Lid in *The 21 Irrefutable Laws of Leadership* states, "Leadership ability determines a person's level of effectiveness." In short, your effectiveness in getting things done and your ability to work through others is always limited by your leadership ability. If your leadership "score" is 4 out of 10, then your effectiveness will be no higher than a 4. Additionally, the Law of Respect says, "People naturally follow leaders stronger than themselves." That means that if you remain a 4, then you will never attract and keep any leaders better than a 3!

One of the burdens of leadership is that as we go, so go the people we lead. Reaching our potential sets an environment for others to reach theirs. When leaders stop climbing, two questions need to be asked: "Can they improve?" and "Will they improve?" Some people can't; they've reached their limit. Others won't. Capacity is not the problem: choice and attitude are. If people are willing to choose improvement and change their attitude, the sky is the limit.

Your leadership ability today is whatever it is. You can't

change the past. However, you can change the future. You have a choice concerning your leadership ability from this day forward. If you learn to climb the Levels of Leadership, your leadership ability will improve. And that will positively impact your overall leadership capacity. However, if you choose not to grow as a leader, you better get used to being wherever you currently are, because your situation isn't likely to improve.

9. When You Change Positions or Organizations, You Seldom Stay at the Same Level

Every time you lead a new person, you start the process over again. People don't recognize you as a Level 4, a People Developer, if you haven't worked with them. You have to earn that. The same goes for Levels 3 and 2. You start over at Level 1. However, there is good news. If you reached Level 4 with some other group of people, you already know how to get there. And because you've done it before, you can move up the levels much more quickly than the previous time.

Each time you go through the process with a new group of people, you become even more skilled at it. And after you've done it enough times, you won't be discouraged by the prospect of having to repeat it with others. Positional leaders are reluctant to have to start over. Because they think of leadership as a destination instead of a process—a noun instead of a verb—they want to hold onto what they have. Their hope is to do it once and be done. Good leaders are willing to re-earn their way back into leadership because they understand that the leadership life will almost always require them to start again at the bottom more than once.

10. You Cannot Climb the Levels Alone

One of my favorite sayings is, "If you think you're leading but no one is following, then you are only taking a walk." That thought captures the true nature of leadership and also expresses the most important insight about the 5 Levels of Leadership. To succeed as a leader, you must help others follow you up the levels. The entire process includes other people and focuses on helping them.

I believe every person has the ability to improve in leadership. Becoming a successful leader isn't a mystical subject. It can be approached very practically, and everyone has the potential to move up to a higher level of leadership.

What is your potential? Do you have the capacity and the desire to become a Level 3, 4, or 5 leader? There's only one way to find out. Accept the leadership challenge, give growth your best effort, and dive into leadership. If you're willing to pick up the gauntlet, you'll never regret it, because there is no better way to increase your positive impact on the world and add value to others than to increase your leadership ability.

I believe this book, with its guides for growth at each level, will help you navigate the process and help you climb. So good reading, good growing, and, as my friend Zig Ziglar says, "I'll see you at the top."

Level 1
POSITION

It's a Great Place to Visit, but You Wouldn't
Want to Live There

Leadership traditionally begins with Position. Someone joins the army, and he or she becomes a recruit, working to earn the rank of private. A person gets a job, and along with it usually comes a title or job description: laborer, salesperson, waiter, clerk, accountant, manager. Position is the starting place for every level of leadership. It is the bottom floor and the foundation upon which leadership must be built. Real influence must be developed upon that foundation. Position gives you a chance, but it usually carries with it very little real power, except in systems where the penalties for not following are dire.

There's nothing wrong with having a position of leadership. When a person receives a leadership position, it's usually because someone in authority saw talent and potential in that person. And with that title and position come some rights and a degree of authority to lead others.

Position is a good starting place. And like every level of leadership, it has its upside and downside. Let's start by looking at the good things about the Position level of leadership.

The Upside of Position

*You Have Been Invited to the
Leadership Table*

Just as there are positive and negative aspects in every season of life, there are both positive and negative aspects to every level of leadership. If you are new to leadership and you receive a position, then there are things to celebrate. I'm going to tell you about four of them.

1. A Leadership Position Is Usually Given to People Because They Have Leadership Potential

Most of the time when people enter a leadership position, they do so because it was granted or appointed by some other person in authority. That probably seems obvious. But think about the implication: It usually means that the person in authority believes the new leader has some degree of potential for leading. That's good news. So if you're new to leadership and you have been invited to lead something, then celebrate the fact that someone in authority believes in you.

The best leaders promote people into leadership based on leadership potential, not on politics, seniority, credentials, or convenience. If you have a new leadership position, then let me say welcome to the first step in your leadership journey. You have a seat at the table and have been invited to be part of the "leadership game." You will have opportunities to express your opinion and make decisions. Your initial goal should be to show your leader and your team that you deserve the position you have received.

Whether you were invited to lead a week or a decade ago, it's never too late to express gratitude to the person who invited you to the leadership table. Take the time to write a note or an e-mail to thank that person and express the positive impact that leading has had on your life.

2. A Leadership Position Means Authority Is Recognized

When an individual receives a position and title, some level of authority or power usually comes with them. Often in the beginning that power is very limited, but that's okay because most leaders need to prove themselves with little before being given much.

As a new leader, you must use the authority you are given wisely, to advance the team and help the people you lead. Do that, and your people will begin to give you even greater authority. When that happens, you gain leadership, not just a position.

3. A Leadership Position Is an Invitation to Grow as a Leader

The journey through the 5 Levels of Leadership will only be successful if you dedicate yourself to continual development. If you believe that the position makes the leader, you will have a hard time becoming a good leader. You will be tempted to stop and "graze," meaning you'll stay where you are and enjoy the position's benefits instead of striving to grow and become the best leader you can. If you want to make an impact, start with yourself.

The leaders who do the greatest harm to an organization are the ones who think they have arrived. Once they receive the title or position they desire, they stop growing. They stop innovating. They stop improving. They rest on their entitlements and clog up everything. Make the most of this opportunity in leadership by making growth your goal. And strive to keep growing. Good leaders are always good learners. To be an effective leader, you must believe that the leadership position you receive is merely an invitation to grow. If you do that and become a lifetime learner, you will continually increase your influence over time. And you will make the most of your leadership potential, no matter how great or small it might be.

4. A Leadership Position Allows Potential Leaders to Shape and Define Their Leadership

The greatest upside potential for people invited to take a leadership position is that it affords them the opportunity to

decide what kind of leader they want to be. The position they
receive may be defined, but they, as people, are not. When
you first become a leader, your leadership page is blank and
you get to fill it in any way you want! What kind of leader
do you want to be? Don't just become reactive and develop
a style by default. Really think about it. Do you want to be
a tyrant or a team builder? Do you want to come down on
people or lift them up? Do you want to give orders or ask
questions? You can develop whatever style you want as long
as it is consistent with who you are.

If you are new to leadership—or new to a particular
leadership position—it is the perfect time to think about the
leadership style you desire to develop. If you are an experienced leader, you can of course reevaluate the way you lead
and make changes. However, you will be working against
your people's past experiences and have to overcome their
expectations.

As you move forward, consider the following three
things:

Who Am I?

Good leadership begins with leaders knowing who they are.
Successful leaders work hard to know themselves. They
know their own strengths and weaknesses. They understand
their own temperament. They know what personal experiences serve them well. They know their work habits as well
as their daily, monthly, and seasonal rhythms. They know
which kinds of people they work well with and which kinds

they have to try harder with to appreciate. They have a sense of where they are going and how they want to get there. As a result, they know what they're capable of doing, and their leadership is steady. Knowing yourself on a pretty deep level isn't quick or easy. It is a long and involved process. Some of it isn't particularly fun. But it is necessary if you want to become a better leader. Self-knowledge is foundational to effective leading.

What Are My Values?

Your values are the soul of your leadership, and they drive your behavior. Before you can grow and mature as a leader, you must have a clear understanding of your values and commit to living consistently with them—since they will shape your behavior and influence the way you lead. As you reflect on your values, I believe you should settle what you believe in three key areas:

- **Ethical Values**—What does it mean to do the right thing for the right reason?
- **Relational Values**—How do you build an environment of trust and respect with others?
- **Success Values**—What goals are worth spending your life on?

If you answer these questions and commit yourself to living your values in these three areas, you'll be well on your way to developing the integrity that makes you attractive to team members and makes them want to follow your leadership.

Immature leaders try to use their position to drive high performance. Mature leaders with self-knowledge realize that consistently high performance from their people isn't prompted by position, power, or rules. It is encouraged by values that are real and genuine.

What Leadership Practices Do I Want to Put into Place?

If you want to become a successful leader, you must not only know yourself and define your values, you must also live them out. You will not grow as a leader unless you commit to getting out of your comfort zone and trying to be a better leader than you are today. Write a declaration of commitment to growth that describes what you will do to grow and how you will approach it. Then sign and date it. Put it someplace where you can reference it in the future. This marks the day you committed to becoming the leader you have the potential to be.

As you think about the way you will define your leadership, take into consideration what kinds of habits and systems you will consistently practice. What will you do to organize yourself? What will you do every day when you arrive at work? What spiritual practices will you maintain to keep yourself on track? How will you treat people? What will be your work ethic? What kind of example will you set? Everything is up for grabs. It's up to you to define it. And the earlier you are on the leadership journey, the greater the potential for gain if you start developing good habits now. (You may want to look at my book *Make Today Count* for the twelve areas I focus on and the habits I use daily to manage my life.)

The bottom line is that an invitation to lead people is an invitation to make a difference. Good leadership changes individual lives. It forms teams. It builds organizations. It impacts communities. It has the potential to impact the world. But never forget that position is only the starting point.

The Downside of Position

True Leadership Isn't about Position

Like everything else in life, the Position level of leadership has negatives as well as positives. Each of the levels of leadership possesses downsides as well as upsides. You will find as you move up the levels that the upsides increase and the downsides decrease. Since Position is the lowest level of leadership, it has a great number of negatives. On Level 1, I see eight major downsides.

1. Having a Leadership Position Is Often Misleading

The easiest way to define leadership is by position. Once you have a position or title, people will identify you with it. However, positions and titles are very misleading. A position always promises more than it can deliver. Having a leadership position does not make you a leader; rather, it is an opportunity to become a leader.

When I received my first position as a pastor I didn't understand that leadership was given to me but not yet earned by me. I arrived at my first meeting to find that a long-standing member of the church had been earning his influence through many positive actions over many years. Even though he did not have the official leadership title, people followed him—not me—as a result. Back then I defined leading as a noun (who I was) not a verb (what I was doing). Leadership is action, not position.

2. Leaders Who Rely on Position to Lead Often Devalue People

People who rely on position for their leadership almost always place a very high value on holding on to their position—often above everything else they do. They often see subordinates as an annoyance, as interchangeable cogs in the organizational machine, or even as troublesome obstacles to their goal of getting a promotion to their next position. As a result, departments, teams, or organizations that have positional leaders suffer terrible morale.

Leaders who rely on their title or position to influence others just do not seem to work well with people. Some don't even like people! They neglect many of the human aspects of leading others. They ignore the fact that all people have hopes, dreams, desires, and goals of their own. They don't recognize that as leaders they must bring together their vision and the aspirations of their people in a way that benefits everyone. In short, they do not lead well because they fail to acknowledge and take into account that leadership—of any kind, in any location, for any purpose—is about working with people.

3. Positional Leaders Feed on Politics

When leaders value position over the ability to influence others, the environment of the organization usually becomes very political. There is a lot of maneuvering. Positional leaders focus on control instead of contribution. They work to gain titles. They do what they can to get the largest staff and the biggest budget they can—not for the sake of the organization's mission but for the sake of expanding and defending their turf. And when a positional leader is able to do this, it often incites others to do the same because they worry that others' gains will be their loss. Not only does this create a vicious cycle of gamesmanship, posturing, and maneuvering; it also creates departmental rivalries and silos.

I have yet to find a highly political organization that runs at top efficiency and possesses high morale. Just look at most of our government institutions and think about the leaders and workers in them. Most people could certainly use improvement, and moving away from positional leadership would do a lot to help them.

4. Positional Leaders Place Rights over Responsibilities

Inevitably, positional leaders who rely on their rights develop a sense of entitlement. They expect their people to serve them; they don't look for ways to serve their people. Their job description is more important to them than job development. They value territory over teamwork. As a result, they usually emphasize rules and regulations that are to their advantage, and they ignore relationships. This does nothing to promote teamwork or create a positive working environment.

Just because you have the right to do something as a leader doesn't mean that it is the right thing to do. Changing your focus from rights to responsibilities is often a sign of maturity in a leader. Many of us were excited in early leadership years by the authority we had and what we could do with it. That power can be exhilarating, if not downright intoxicating. Each of us as leaders must strive to grow up and grow into a leadership role without relying on our rights. If we can mature in that way, we will start to change our focus from enjoying authority for its own sake to using authority to serve others.

5. Positional Leadership Is Often Lonely

Being a good leader doesn't mean trying to be king of the hill and standing above (and apart from) others. Good leadership is about walking beside people and helping them to climb up the hill with you. King-of-the-hill leaders create a negative work environment because they are insecure and easily threatened. Whenever they see people with potential starting to climb, it worries them. They fear that their place on top is being threatened. As a result, they undermine the people who show talent, trying to guard their position and keep themselves clearly above and ahead of anyone else. What is the usual result? The best people, feeling undermined and put down, leave the department or organization and look for another hill to climb. Only average or unmotivated people stay. And they know their place is at the bottom. That develops an us-versus-them culture, with the positional leader standing alone on top. Leadership doesn't have to be lonely. People who feel lonely have created a situation that makes them feel that way. If you're atop the hill alone, you may get lonely. If you have others alongside you, it's hard to be that way.

6. Leaders Who Remain Positional Get Branded and Stranded

Whenever people use their position to lead others for a long time and fail to develop genuine influence, they become branded as positional leaders, and they rarely get further opportunities for advancement in that organization. They may move laterally, but they rarely move up.

If you have been a positional leader, you can change, and this book will help you. However, you need to recognize that the longer you have relied on your position, the more difficult it will be for you to change others' perceptions about your leadership style. You may even need to change positions in order to restart the process of developing influence with others.

7. Turnover Is High for Positional Leaders

When people rely on their positions for leadership, the result is almost always high turnover. Good leaders leave an organization when they have to follow bad leaders. Good workers leave an organization when the work environment is poor. Interview people who have left and the odds are high that they did not leave a *job*. They left the people they had to work with.

Every company has turnover. It is inevitable. The question every leader must ask is, "Who is leaving?" Organizations with Level 1 leadership tend to lose their best people and attract average or below-average people. The more Level 1 leaders an organization has, the more the door swings out with high-level people and in with low-level people.

An organization will not function on a level higher than its leader. It just doesn't happen. If a Level 1 leader is in charge, the organization will eventually be a Level 1 organization. If the leader is on Level 4, then the organization will never get to Level 5—unless the leader grows to that level.

8. Positional Leaders Receive People's Least, Not Their Best

People who rely on their positions and titles are the weakest of all leaders. They give their least. They expect their position to do the hard work for them in leadership. As a result, their people also give their least. Some people who work for a positional leader may start out strong, ambitious, innovative, and motivated, but they rarely stay that way. Typically, they become one of the following three types of people.

Clock Watchers

Followers who thrive in Level 1 leadership environments love clocks, and they want them visible at all times throughout the building. They evaluate every moment at work according to the clock: how long they've been there, how much time they have left, how long until break time, and how long until lunchtime. Clock watchers always know how much time is left before they get to go home, and they never want to work a moment beyond quitting time. But think about it: when the people who work with you can hardly wait to quit working with you, something is not working!

"Just-Enough" Employees

When leaders use their leadership position as leverage, the people who work for them often begin to rely on their rights as employees and the limits of their job descriptions to protect them from having to work any more than is absolutely necessary. They do only what's required of them. They do just enough—to get by, to get paid, and to keep their job. When people follow a leader because they have to, they will do only what they have to. People don't give their best to leaders they like least. They give reluctant compliance, not commitment. They may give their hands but certainly not their heads or hearts. "Just-enough" people have a hard time showing up. The only commitment they show is to taking off the maximum days allowed for any reason. Some spend a lot of mental energy finding creative ways of eliminating work. If only they used that commitment in positive ways!

The Mentally Absent

In a Level 1 environment, there are always individuals who may be physically present but mentally absent. They do not engage mentally, and they show up merely to collect a paycheck. This attitude is highly damaging to an organization because it seems to spread. When one person checks out mentally and doesn't suffer any consequences for it, others often follow. Mental turnover and sloppiness are contagious. When the people who work for a team, a department, or an organization give little of themselves, the results are mediocre at best. And morale is abysmal. Success demands more than most people are willing to offer, but not more than they are capable of giving. The thing that often makes the difference is good leadership. That is not found on Level 1.

The greatest downside about Level 1 leadership is that it is neither creative nor innovative. It's leadership that just gets by. And if a leader stays on the downside of Level 1 long enough, he may find himself on the outside. If a leader fails on Level 1, there's nowhere to go but U-Haul territory. He'll be moving out and looking for another job.

Best Behaviors on Level 1

How to Make the Most of Your Position

All leaders can learn to lead differently and move up the levels of leadership if they're willing to change the way they lead on Level 1. How do you make the most of your leadership position while shifting from positional to permissional leadership?

1. Stop Relying on Position to Push People

There is nothing wrong with having a leadership position. That's the starting place for most leadership. However, there is everything wrong with having a positional mind-set. If you have to tell people that you're the leader, you're not. If you continue to rely on your position to move people, you may never develop influence with them, and your success will always be limited.

Level 1 leaders think:

Top-down—"I'm over you."
Separation—"Don't let people get close to you."
Image—"Fake it till you make it."
Strength—"Never let 'em see you sweat."
Selfishness—"You're here to help me."

Power—"I determine your future."
Intimidation—"Do this or else!"
Rules—"The manual says..."

By contrast, higher-level leaders think differently. Level 2 leaders think in terms of:

Collaboration—"Let's work together."
Initiation—"I'll come to you."
Inclusion—"What do you think?"
Cooperation—"Together we can win."
Service—"I'm here to help you."
Development—"I want to add value to you."
Encouragement—"I believe you can do this!"
Innovation—"Let's think outside the box."

Level 2 relies on people skills, not power, to get things done. It treats individual followers as people, not mere subordinates. If you want to become a better leader, let go of control and start fostering cooperation. Good leaders stop bossing people around and start encouraging them. That is the secret to being a people-oriented leader, because much of successful leadership is encouragement.

2. Trade Entitlement for Movement

Good leaders don't take anything for granted. They keep working and keep leading. They understand that leadership must be earned and established. They remain dissatisfied in a way, because dissatisfaction is a good one-word definition of "motivation." Good leaders strive to keep the people and the organization moving forward toward its vision. They recognize that organizations can sometimes be filled with appointees, but teams can be built only by good leadership.

You may have been appointed to a Level 1 position, but you will have to lead yourself and others above it. You must be willing to give up what is in order to reach for what could be. Let a vision for making a difference lift you and your people above the confines of job descriptions and petty rules. Forget about your leadership rights. Focus on your responsibility to make a difference in the lives of the people you lead. When you receive a position or title, you haven't arrived. It's time to start moving—and taking others along with you.

Leadership isn't a right. It's a privilege. It must be continually earned. If you possess any sense of entitlement, that will work against you. If you've thought in terms of position, change your focus. Instead, think about your leadership potential. What kind of leader do you have the potential to become? What kind of positive effect can you have on the people you lead? What kind of impact can you make on the world? Rewrite your goals to embrace a nonpositional mind-set. It will make a difference in your teachability and the way you treat your team members.

3. Leave Your Position and Move toward Your People

People who rely on position often mistakenly believe that it is the responsibility of the people to come to them for what they need and want. Good leaders understand that it is their responsibility to move toward their people. Leaders are initiators.

The Greek philosopher Socrates said, "Let him that would move the world first move himself." If you want to move up to Level 2 in your leadership, you need to get out of your territory. You need to stop being king of the hill, get down from your high place, and find your people. You must move beyond your job description, both in terms of the work you do and the way you interact with your people. You must make it your responsibility to learn who they are, find out what they need, and help them and the team win.

In order to do anything new in life, we must be willing to leave our comfort zone. That involves taking risks, which can be frightening. However, each time we leave our comfort zone and conquer new territory, it not only expands our comfort zone but also enlarges us. If you want to grow as a leader, be prepared to be uncomfortable. But know this: the risks are well worth the rewards.

Beliefs That Help a Leader Move Up to Level 2

To change from a Level 1 leader to a Level 2 leader, you must first change the way you think about leadership. No one has to remain a positional leader, though the longer you have relied on your position, the longer it may take you to change the way you lead and the way others see you. You will have to earn your way up from Level 1.

Here are four statements you must embrace internally before you will be able to change from a positional leader to a permissional one.

1. Titles Are Not Enough

We live in a culture that values titles. We admire and respect people with titles such as doctor, CEO, chairman, PhD, Academy Award winner, director, Nobel Prize winner, salesman of the year, president, poet laureate. But titles are ultimately empty, and you must learn to see them that way. Who the person is and the work he does are what really matter. People who make career goals out of attaining certain titles are not setting themselves up to be the best leaders they can be.

If the work is significant and adds value to people, then it doesn't need to come with a title. For every person who has received recognition, there are thousands of others working without recognition who perhaps deserve even greater honor. Yet they continue to work without credit because the work itself and the positive impact on others are reward enough.

Developing an awareness that titles have little real value and that Position is the lowest level of leadership brings a healthy sense of dissatisfaction with Level 1 as well as a desire to grow. A position is not a worthy destination for any person's life. Security does not give purpose. Leadership is meant to be active and dynamic. Its purpose is to create positive change. Do whatever you have to do to identify less with your title and position and more with how you contribute to the team or organization.

2. People—Not Positions—Are a Leader's Most Valuable Asset

If you want to become a better leader, you can't focus on rules and procedures to get things done or keep things going. You must develop relationships. People get things done, not the playbook they use.

It takes some time to develop the people skills needed to become a better leader, but it takes no time at all to let others know that you value them, to express appreciation for them, and to take interest in them personally. So that's a change you can make quickly. Go out of your way to communicate how much you value each person you lead. People are the most valuable and appreciable asset of any organization. You must be certain to treat them that way. And here's the immediate benefit: the moment people notice the shift in your attitude, you'll notice a positive shift in their response to you. They'll begin to help you, which allows you to help them.

3. A Leader Doesn't Need to Have All the Answers

Positional leaders often believe that they need to have all the answers. After all, if they admit that they don't know something, it shows weakness. And if they show weakness, how are they going to stay on top of the hill and maintain their precious position? To get off of Level 1, a leader has to think differently.

A leader's job is not to know everything but to attract people who know things that he or she does not. One of us is not as smart as all of us. Stop bringing people together to give them the answers and start calling on them to help you find the answers. That will transform your leadership, not only because you can be yourself and stop pretending that you know more than you do but also because it harnesses the power of shared thinking.

When people ask you something that you don't know, admit it. Then ask for the opinions of the people on your team. If they don't have the answers to questions, ask them if they know people who do. Make problem solving collaborative.

4. A Good Leader Always Includes Others

Because positional leaders often work alone, standing atop the hill of leadership while their subordinates work together at the bottom, their teams work far below their capabilities. Why? Stand-alone leadership doesn't lead to teamwork, creativity, collaboration, or high achievement. What a shame, and what a waste of potential.

Successful leadership is all about others. It means relating well to other people. It requires leaders to be examples for other people. It challenges them to develop and equip people. The higher you go up the levels of leadership, the more you realize that good leadership is about leading *with* others, not just leading others. It requires collaboration. It requires inclusion. It requires sacrifice of selfish personal ambition for the sake of the team and the vision of the organization. It means being part of something greater than yourself. It means putting others ahead of yourself and being willing to go only as fast as the people you lead.

Moving up from Level 1 to Level 2 requires the greatest personal change from a leader. It requires a change of beliefs and attitudes toward other people and leadership. But here's the truth: once you decide to include others in the leadership journey, you are well on your way to achieving success at the other levels.

Level 2
PERMISSION
*You Can't Lead People until
You Like People*

When a leader learns to function on the Permission level, people do more than merely comply with orders. They actually start to follow. And they do so because they really want to. Why? Because the leader begins to influence people with relationships, not just position. Relationships are a major key to success, whether you're trying to sell, coach, teach, lead, or simply navigate the daily tasks of life. Building relationships develops a foundation for effectively leading others. It also starts to break down organizational silos as people connect across the lines between their job descriptions or departments. The more barriers come down and relationships deepen, the broader the foundation for leading others becomes. When people feel liked, cared for, included, valued, and trusted, they begin to work together with their leader and each other. And that can change the entire working environment. The old saying is really true: people go along with leaders they get along with.

Moving up to Level 2 is an important development in leadership because that is where followers give their supervisors permission to lead them. People change from being subordinates to followers for the first time, and that means there is movement! Remember, leadership always means that people are going somewhere. They aren't static. No journey, no leadership.

The Upside of Permission

The Workplace Has Become More Pleasant for Everyone

There are many upsides to Level 2 because the focus on relationship building opens up so many new avenues of leadership. Here are my top five upsides.

1. Leadership Permission Makes Work More Enjoyable

Level 2 leaders like people and treat them like individuals. They develop relationships and win people over with interaction instead of using the power of their position. They shift their focus from "me" to "we." That attitude creates a positive working environment. The workplace becomes more friendly. People begin to like each other. Chemistry starts to develop on the team. People no longer possess a "have to" mind-set. Instead it turns to "want to." The workplace becomes more enjoyable for everyone—leaders and followers alike. Permissional leaders want to help people. They want to see them succeed. The prevalent attitude is one of serving others and bringing out the best in the people they work with.

2. Leadership Permission Increases the Energy Level

What happens when you spend time with people you don't especially like or who don't like you? Doesn't it drain you of energy? That kind of environment brings most people down. Even in a neutral environment, if you are with people you don't know very well, doesn't it require a lot of energy to get to know them? Connecting with others always takes energy. Conversely, what happens when you spend time with people you know and like? Doesn't it give you energy? I know it does for me. Spending time with the people I love—whether at work, at home, or while playing—is my greatest joy, and it always energizes me.

Good relationships create energy, and they give people's interaction a positive tone. When you invest time and effort to get to know people and build good relationships, it actually pays off with greater energy once the relationships are built. And in that kind of positive, energetic environment, people are willing to give their best because they know the leader wants the best for them.

3. Leadership Permission Opens Up Channels of Communication

The Permission level requires and cultivates good communication and side-by-side relationships. Level 2 leaders listen to their people, and their people listen to them. I believe most leaders are naturally better at talking than listening. I know that was true for me when I was early in my leadership journey. I was intent on communicating my vision to others and making sure they understood my agenda. I wanted communication to go only one way—from me to them. The result was that few people bought into my leadership or my vision. I failed to realize that the road to vision buy-in was two-way communication. That meant I had to learn how to listen.

When you open up the channels of communication on Level 2 and really listen, here is what you must give others:

Ears—"I hear what you say."
Eyes—"I see what you say."
Heart—"I feel what you say."
Undivided attention—"I value who you are and what you say."

Only when we do these things are we able to build positive relationships and persuade people to follow us.

When leaders forge relationships on Level 2, they not only create better communication, they also create an environment where people begin to work together in a spirit of community and to communicate with one another openly.

4. Leadership Permission Focuses on the Value of Each Person

Level 2 leadership is relationally driven. That is only possible when people respect and value one another. It is impossible to relate well with those you don't respect. When respect lessens in a relationship, the relationship diminishes. You can care for people without leading them, but you cannot lead them effectively beyond Level 1 without caring for them.

Nothing lifts a person like being respected and valued by others. As a leader on Level 2, your goals should be to become aware of the uniqueness of people and learn to appreciate their differences. You need to let them know that they matter, that you see them as individual human beings, not just workers. This attitude makes a positive impact on people, and it strengthens your leadership and the organization.

To evaluate where you are with your team, write a list of the names of the people on your team. Then determine how well you know each of them by answering the following questions (which come from materials Eli Lilly and Company developed based on the 5 Levels of Leadership):

- What three nonbusiness things do you know about this person?
- What does this person value?
- What are this person's top three concerns?
- What does this person want or hope for in life?

If you are unable to answer these questions for someone on your team, then you need to set aside time to get to know him or her better.

5. Leadership Permission Nurtures Trust

If you have integrity with people, you develop trust. Trust is the foundation of Permission. The more trust you develop, the stronger the relationship becomes. The better the relationship, the greater the potential for a leader to gain permission to lead. It's a building process that takes time, energy, and intentionality.

Retired admiral James Stockdale said, "When the crunch comes, people cling to those they know they can trust—those who are not detached, but involved." That is the power of Permission. In times of difficulty, relationships are a shelter. In times of opportunity, they are a launching pad. Trust is required for people to feel safe enough to create, share, question, attempt, and risk. Without it, leadership is weak and teamwork is impossible.

The Downside of Permission

The Pressure Is on You to Build Positive Relationships

If you're a relational person, as I am, you may be saying to yourself, *What downside can there possibly be to developing relationships, building trust, and gaining people's permission to lead? Isn't it all good?* My answer has to be no. While it is true that the positives far outweigh the negatives, there are still downsides to Level 2. Here are the ones I have observed.

1. Permission Leadership Appears Too Soft for Some People

In a hard-charging, high-performance, leadership-intensive environment, leading by permission may appear "soft" to some people. Caring for people and being relational can be seen as weak, especially by leaders who possess a natural bias toward action rather than affection. For that reason, some people dismiss it. What a mistake—and what a handicap to their leadership potential.

It's been my observation that most people start their

leadership focused on either the "hard" aspects of leadership, meaning the productivity side, or on the "soft" aspects, meaning the relational side. Those who start on the hard side and refuse to learn softer skills often get stuck on Level 1. They desire to go to Level 3, Production, but they can't achieve it without learning and earning Level 2 first.

In contrast, those who start on the soft side gladly and easily work their way up to Level 2, Permission, but if they don't do more than just win relationships, they get stuck and never move up to Level 3, Production, either. It takes both Permission and Production to become a good leader.

If you're relational without being productive, you and your team won't achieve any progress. If you're productive without being relational, you may make a small degree of progress in the beginning, but you'll fall short in the long run because you'll either alienate your people or burn them out. You can't become successful in leadership until you learn both.

2. Leading by Permission Can Be Frustrating for Achievers

High achievers want to get things done and get them done now! They usually don't want to slow down for anything or anyone. Leading by permission requires them to do exactly that. Building relationships takes time. It can be very slow work.

If at one end of the spectrum you have achievers ignoring

relationships, at the other end you have highly relational people who allow the relationships to become an end unto themselves. That's not healthy, either. In fact, the most common reason for leaders not moving up to Level 3 is that they become so relational that they lose sight of the primary goal of leadership: helping others to work together, move forward, and achieve. When relationships become an end unto themselves, then high-achieving followers who focus on bottom-line results become restless and often try to do one of two things: take over or leave. You must win both levels as a leader to be successful.

As long as you're winning, people are willing to follow—even if you are hard on them or positional in your leadership. However, when you drive people to achieve without slowing down to build relationships, a part of them will want to see you lose. There's a saying that if you step on people's fingers on the way up, they may trip you on the way down. At the very least, if you fail, they'll celebrate your fall and then move on.

3. Permissional Leaders Can Be Taken Advantage Of

People whose leadership style is nonrelational are usually seen as no-nonsense leaders. Positional leaders often use their positions to distance themselves from subordinates. High achievers sometimes intimidate their followers. But when leaders are relational, their followers naturally get closer to them. That sometimes means that they mistake kindness for weakness. They believe that encouragement means they don't have to respect boundaries. They assume that empowerment means they have the freedom to do whatever they want. As a result, they take advantage of their leaders.

As you build relationships with people on Level 2, I believe you will find that there are four kinds of people:

- **Takers,** who leverage the relationship to better themselves but not you or anyone else. They borrow your influence but keep the return.
- **Developers,** who leverage the relationship in a positive way, bettering themselves and you.
- **Acquaintances,** who are content to live off of their relationship with you passively, benefiting from successes but never contributing or taking responsibility to grow themselves.
- **Friends,** who enjoy their relationship with you, returning your goodwill and never taking unfair advantage of it.

Being relational is a risk, just as opening yourself up to falling in love is a risk. Sure, you can stay guarded and never get hurt. But you will also never have the chance to have deep, rewarding relationships that will enrich your life and the lives of others.

4. Permission Leadership Requires Openness to Be Effective

Most people don't want to admit their mistakes, expose their faults, and face up to their shortcomings. They don't want their flaws to be discovered. They don't get too close to people because of the negatives in their lives. And if people receive a leadership position, the urge to hide their weaknesses can become even stronger. Most people believe they must show greater strength as leaders. However, if leaders try to maintain a facade with the people they lead, they cannot build authentic relationships.

To develop authentic relationships on the Permission level, leaders need to be authentic. They must admit their mistakes. They must own up to their faults. They must recognize their shortcomings. In other words, they must be the real deal. That is a vulnerable place to be for a leader. And truthfully, it is one of the main reasons many leaders never progress from Level 1 to Level 2 in leadership.

5. Permission Leadership Is Difficult for People Who Are Not Naturally Likable

Some individuals are naturally gifted with people. They interact well with others and easily develop relationships. But what about people who are not naturally gifted at working with people? For them, moving up to Level 2 usually doesn't come as easily. If they want to win Permission with others, they have to work to make themselves more likable. If you find that difficult, how can you do it? By doing the following:

- If you haven't already, make a choice to care about others. Liking people and caring about people is a choice within your control.

- Look for something that is likable about every person you meet. It's there. Make it your job to find it.
- Discover what is likable about yourself and do whatever you can to share that with every person you meet.
- Make the effort every day to express what you like about every person in your life.

If you want to win people's permission and lead effectively on Level 2, you must like people and become more likable yourself.

6. Permission Leadership Forces You to Deal with the Whole Person

Auto pioneer Henry Ford once asked, "Why is it that I always get the whole person when what I really want is a pair of hands?" Let's face it: relationships are messy. Many leaders would rather deal with people only in terms of their work life. But the reality is that when you lead someone, you always get the whole person—including their dysfunctions, home life, health issues, and quirks. Good leaders understand that the heart of leadership is dealing with people and working with the good, the bad, and the ugly in everyone.

The messiness of people problems is what can make leadership no fun. So often, as we get to know others and we start to see their flaws, we become disillusioned with them. Each of us has imperfections and irritating habits. We all fail. So we must learn to accept that about one another and still work together.

As a leader, you may be tempted to build relationships only with the people you like, or with whom you are highly compatible, and to ignore the others. However, by doing that, you have the potential to lose a lot of people. It's important to remember that while the things we have in common may make relationships enjoyable, the differences are what really make them interesting. Good leaders on Level 2 deal successfully with these differences and leverage them for the benefit of the team and organization. They understand that conflict is a part of progress. Often it is even constructive. Good leaders are able to look at hard truths, see people's flaws, face reality, and do it in a spirit of grace and truth. They don't avoid problems; they solve them.

The bottom line on Level 2 is that most of the downsides of leadership come from dealing with people. If you care about people and understand them, then you expect things not to go smoothly. If you go into leadership on the Permission level with that expectation, it frees you to lead with a positive attitude and an open mind. You know that as long as people still have a pulse, you will be dealing with messy and difficult situations.

Best Behaviors on Level 2

How to Gain People's Permission

If you find yourself in a place where you need to start working to win people's permission on Level 2, do the following.

1. Connect with Yourself Before Trying to Connect with Others

One of the secrets of connecting with people and building relationships is knowing and liking yourself. To become someone who is good at building relationships with others, you must become the kind of person you would want to spend time with. There are five components of connecting with yourself:

Self-Awareness—Know your personality type, temperament, talents, strengths, and weaknesses.

Self-Image—Deal with any personal issues you may have so that you can think of yourself in a positive way.

Self-Honesty—Look at yourself realistically and decide to face reality, no matter how much it may hurt.

Self-Improvement—Make a commitment to grow in your ability to develop relationships.

Self-Responsibility—Acknowledge that you are responsible for your own actions and attitudes.

Every significant accomplishment begins with one person stepping up and committing to make a difference. That person then takes responsibility to pass it on to others. If you don't take responsibility for yourself, then don't expect your life to become any different from what it is right now.

2. Develop a People-Oriented Leadership Style

Permissional leaders don't rely on rules to lead people. They don't depend on systems. And they never try to rule with a stick. (Anyone who does needs to know that every stick eventually breaks.) Instead, they use a personal touch whenever they deal with people. They listen, learn, and then lead. They develop relationships. They have more than an open-door policy—they know the door swings both ways. They go through it and get out among their people to connect.

Good leaders never take people out of the equation in anything they do. They always take people into account— where they are, what they believe, what they're feeling. Every question they ask is expressed in the context of people. Knowing what to do isn't enough to make someone a good leader. Just because something is right doesn't necessarily mean that people will let you do it. Good leaders take that into account. And they think and plan accordingly.

If you want to be successful on Level 2, you must think more in terms of people's emotions and human capacity and less in terms of systems and regulations. You must think more in terms of buy-in and less in terms of procedures. In other words, you must think of people before you try to achieve progress. Exhibit a consistent mood, maintain an optimistic attitude, possess a listening ear, and present to others your authentic self.

3. Practice the Golden Rule

There is a fine line between manipulating people and motivating them. I agree that leaders who put an emphasis on motivating people can use leadership for personal gain at the expense of others. However, a permissional leader can keep that tendency in check and keep from crossing over from motivation to manipulation by following the golden rule: *Treat others as you would like to be treated.*

The golden rule cuts across cultural and religious boundaries and is embraced by people from nearly every part of the world. Practicing the golden rule in leadership enables everyone to feel respected. That changes the entire environment of a department or an organization. When leaders change from driving people in a positional environment to respecting people in a permissional environment, their people go from feeling like a stake to feeling like a stakeholder.

4. Become the Chief Encourager
of Your Team

As a leader, you have great power to lift people up. People enjoy affirmation from a peer. But they really value it from their leader. The words "I'm glad you work with me; you add incredible value to the team" mean a lot coming from someone who has the best interest of the team, department, or organization at heart.

If you want people to be positive and to always be glad when they see you coming, encourage them. People are naturally attracted to people who give them confidence and make them feel good about themselves. You can be a leader who does that if you're willing to become an intentional encourager. Try it out. For the next two weeks, say something encouraging to someone on your team every day. Then watch to see how the person responds. Do that with everyone on your team, and they will not only want to work with you, but they will also get more done.

5. Strike a Balance between Care and Candor

Some people think that succeeding in permissional leadership means treating the people on their team as though they were family. That is almost always a mistake. People don't deal realistically with their families. I don't. I have a commitment level with them that is deeper than with others. Regardless of what my family does, I am committed to giving them unconditional love. They have privileges that I extend to no other people. And compromise is a constant. (Anyone who says they don't believe in compromise has never been married—or stayed married.) What makes a family great isn't what makes a team great. Families value community over contribution. Businesses value contribution over community. The best teams strike a balance.

Other people think that being a permissional leader means giving team members permission to do whatever they want. That idea is also wrong. Just because you care about people doesn't mean you let them work without responsibility or accountability.

If you care about people, treat them with respect, and build positive relationships with them, you actually have more numerous opportunities to speak candidly and have hard conversations with them that will help them to grow and perform better. Every person has problems and makes mistakes in the workplace. Every person needs to improve and needs someone to come alongside them to help them improve. As a leader, it is your responsibility and your privilege to be the person who helps others get better by balancing care and candor. Care without candor creates dysfunctional relationships. Candor without care creates distant relationships. But care balanced with candor creates developing relationships.

Here's how care and candor work together to help a leader succeed.

Caring Values the Person
While Candor Values the Person's Potential

Caring for others demonstrates that you value them. However, if you want to help people get better, you have to be
honest about where they need to improve. That shows that
you value a person's potential. That requires candor.

One of the secrets of being candid is to think, speak, and
act in terms of those who have the potential for growth and
to think about how you can help them improve. If you're
candid with others with their benefit in mind, it doesn't have
to be harmful. It can be similar to the work of a surgeon. It
may hurt, but it is meant to help and it shouldn't harm. As a
leader, you must be willing and able to do that. If not, you
won't be able to help your people grow and change.

Caring Establishes the Relationship
While Candor Expands the Relationship

The things that usually help to establish a relationship are
common ground and care. But those things usually aren't
enough to make a relationship grow. To expand a relationship, candor and open communication are required. Most
leaders I talk to have a difficult conversation that they know
they need to have but are avoiding. Usually they are reluctant
for one of two reasons: either they don't like confrontation,
or they fear that they will hurt the person they need to talk
to. But if a leader can balance care and candor, it will actually deepen and strengthen the relationship.

Not everyone responds well to candid conversations. Let's face it: honesty can hurt. Some people shut down when you criticize them. Others leave and work somewhere else. However, if you have candid conversations with someone who hangs in there and grows, that person becomes a candidate for the climb up to Level 3 and beyond.

Caring Defines the Relationship
While Candor Directs the Relationship

Solid relationships are defined by how people care about one another. But just because people care about one another doesn't mean that they are going anywhere together. Getting the team moving together to accomplish a goal is the responsibility of the leader, and that often requires candor. Getting results always matters, and good leaders never lose track of that. Retired army general and former secretary of state Colin Powell noted, "Good leadership involves responsibility to the welfare of the group, which means that some people will get angry at your actions and decisions. It's inevitable—if you're honorable." If you want to lead people well, you need to be willing to direct them candidly.

Caring Should Never Suppress Candor
While Candor Should Never Displace Caring

The bottom line is that good leaders must embrace both care and candor. To help you keep the balance between the two, I've created a "caring candor" checklist. Before having a candid conversation, make sure that you can answer yes to the following questions:

- Have I invested enough in the relationship to be candid with this person?
- Do I truly value this person as an individual?
- Am I sure this is his or her issue and not mine?
- Am I sure I'm not speaking up because I feel threatened?
- Is the issue more important than the relationship?
- Does this conversation clearly serve this person's interests and not just mine?
- Am I willing to invest time and energy to help this person change?
- Am I willing to show this person how to do something, and not just say what's wrong?
- Am I willing and able to set clear, specific expectations?

If you can answer yes to all of these questions, then your motives are probably right and you have a good chance of being able to communicate effectively.

The next time you find yourself in a place where you need to have a candid conversation, just remember this:

- Do it quickly—shovel the pile while it's small.
- Do it calmly, never in anger—use the caring candor checklist.

- Do it privately—you want to help the person, not embarrass him or her.
- Do it thoughtfully, in a way that minimizes embarrassment or intimidation.

If your goal is to help the individual, improve the team, and fulfill the vision of the organization, then this is the path you should follow as a leader.

As you work with people and have candid conversations, allow me to remind you of one more thing: candor is a two-way street. If you want to be an effective leader, you must allow the people you work with to be candid with you. You must solicit feedback. And you must be mature and secure enough to take in people's criticism without defensiveness and learn from it. Caring for people, making good decisions for everyone involved, and building solid relationships is what Level 2 is all about. This is Permission at its best.

Beliefs That Help a Leader Move Up to Level 3

Most of the people who fail to move up in leadership don't make it because they never understand the importance of building relationships with the people they work with and gaining their permission to lead them. The Permission level is foundational to good leadership, but it is not your ultimate goal. If you have gained the confidence of those you lead, and are recognized as a person who cares about them, then it's time to start thinking the way a Level 3 leader does. To begin that shift, keep in mind the following three things.

1. Relationships Alone Are Not Enough

Although the Permission level may bring you and your team great satisfaction relationally, if you stay on Level 2 and never advance, you won't really prove yourself as a leader. The good news is that if you've connected with your team, you now have some influence with them. The question now is: What are you going to do with that influence? True leadership takes people somewhere so that they can accomplish something. That requires a leader to connect people's potential to their performance.

2. Building Relationships Requires Twofold Growth

For relationships to be meaningful, people must not only grow toward each other but also grow with each other. Growing toward each other requires compatibility. Growing with each other requires intentionality.

If you are married or in a significant long-term relationship, then you probably understand how these dynamics come into play. When you first met your partner, you moved toward one another, based on attraction, common ground, and shared experiences. You established the relationship. However, a relationship can't last if you never go beyond those initial experiences. To stay together, you need to sustain the relationship. That requires common growth. If you don't grow together, there's a very good chance you may grow apart. Similarly, if you are to have any staying power as a leader, you must grow toward and with your people. Just because you've developed good relationships with your people, don't think that you're done on the relational side. There is still more work to do.

3. Achieving Vision as a Team Is Worth Risking Relationships

Building relationships with people can be hard work. But to succeed as a leader, you have to be willing to risk what you've developed relationally for the sake of the bigger picture. Leaders must be willing to sacrifice for the sake of the vision. If achieving a vision is worth building a team, it is also worth risking your relationships. Building relationships and then risking them to advance the team creates tension for a leader. That tension will force you to make a choice: shrink the vision or stretch the people to reach it.

If you want to do big things, you need to take people out of their comfort zones. They might fail. They might implode. They might relieve their own tension by fighting you or quitting. Risk always changes relationships. If you risk and win, then your people gain confidence. You have shared history that makes the relationship stronger. Trust increases. And the team is ready to take on even more difficult challenges. However, if you risk and fail, you lose relational credibility with your people and you will have to rebuild the relationships. Risk is always present in leadership. Anytime you try to move forward, there is risk. Even if you're doing the right things, your risk isn't reduced. But there is no progress without risk, so you need to get used to it.

The bottom line is that you can slow down early in your leadership to build relationships on Level 2, or you can forge ahead, trying to skip straight to Level 3—but if you do, you will have to backtrack later to build those relationships. And you need to recognize that doing so will slow your momentum, and it can actually take you longer to build the team than if you did it the right way in the first place.

The key link between people and the company is the leader they work with! That leader is the face, heart, and hands of the company on a day-to-day basis. If that leader connects and cares, that makes a huge difference.

Level 3
PRODUCTION

*Making Things Happen Separates Real
Leaders from Wannabes*

The Production level is where leadership really takes off and shifts into another gear. Production qualifies and separates true leaders from people who merely occupy leadership positions. Good leaders always make things happen. They get results. They can make a significant impact on an organization. Not only are they productive individually, they also are able to help the team produce. This ability gives Level 3 leaders confidence, credibility, and increased influence.

No one can fake Level 3. Either you're producing for the organization and adding to its bottom line (whatever that may be) or you're not. Level 3 leaders are self-motivated and productive. As a result, they create momentum and develop an environment of success, which makes the team better and stronger.

Another benefit of leadership on Level 3 is that it attracts other highly productive people. Producers are attractive to other producers. They respect one another. They enjoy collaborating. They get things done together. That ultimately creates growth for the organization.

Some people never move up from Level 2, Permission, to Level 3, Production. Why? They can't seem to produce results. When that is the case, it's usually because they lack the self-discipline, work ethic, organization, or skills to be productive. However, if you desire to go to higher levels of leadership, you simply have to produce. There is no other way around it.

The Upside of Production

You Now Have Leadership Credibility

With the addition of Production, leadership really begins to hit its stride. Having built a foundation of strong relationships, leaders who get results dramatically improve their team and organization. There are so many upsides to Level 3. Here are six of them.

1. Leadership Production Gives Credibility to the Leader

The ability to produce results has always been the line people must be able to cross to be successful. That line is also what qualifies someone for leadership. Peter Drucker, often described as the father of modern management, expressed it this way: "There are two types of people in the business community: those who produce results and those who give you reasons why they didn't."

Authentic leaders know the way and show the way to productivity. They take their people where they want them to go—they don't send them there. They are more like tour guides than travel agents. They live on their performance, not their potential. They lead by example. And their ability to get results tends to silence their critics and build their reputations. People admire and usually welcome achievers who deliver the goods—who get results.

2. Leadership Production Models and Sets the Standard for Others

Productive leaders set an example for the people they lead, and their productivity sets the standard for the team. President Abraham Lincoln recognized this. During the American Civil War, the president relieved General John C. Frémont of his command. He said it was for this reason: "His cardinal mistake is that he isolates himself and allows no one to see him." Lincoln knew that leaders need to be among their people, inspiring them with their abilities, letting them see what the standard should be for their performance.

Some leaders make the same mistake as some parents. They expect people to do as they say, not as they do. But here's the problem: people do what people see. If you want dedicated, thoughtful, productive people on your team, you must embody those characteristics.

Take time to list all the qualities you desire in your team members. Then compare your own personal qualities to those on the list. Wherever you desire a quality in others that you don't possess yourself, create an action statement describing what you must do to possess the trait you'd like to see.

3. Leadership Production Brings Clarity and Reality to the Vision

Good leaders constantly communicate the vision of the organization. They do it clearly, creatively, and continually. But that doesn't mean that everyone who receives the message understands and embraces it. The Production level of leadership communicates the vision through action, which helps people understand it in ways they may not have before. When followers see positive results and see goals being met, they get a clearer picture of what it means to fulfill the vision.

Level 3 leaders help their people see what productivity looks like. And with each day of productivity, the team gets one step closer to making the vision a reality. That encourages members of the team. It validates their efforts. It makes the vision that much clearer. And clarity is compelling. Productivity also expands the vision, because with increased confidence and skill, the people doing the work recognize that they can actually accomplish more than they may have believed was possible.

4. Leadership Production Solves a Multitude of Problems

Many people in leadership positions try to solve problems by using systems. Or they pay others to try to solve problems for them. But the truth is, leaders cannot delegate the solving of problems to someone else. They have to be active in breaking through obstacles, putting out fires, correcting mistakes, and directing people. Leaders on the Production level do that. And once their effectiveness becomes contagious and spreads throughout the team, productivity begins to solve many problems—many more than managers or consultants ever will.

Productive organizations led by Level 3 leaders are hard to beat. Their effectiveness is high, and so is their morale. Productivity is inspiring. People who feel good about themselves often produce good results.

5. Leadership Production Creates Momentum

When well-led organizations sustain high morale and high productivity over time, they gain momentum, which is any leader's best friend. Momentum helps a leader do anything and everything more easily. That's why I call it the great exaggerator. Without momentum, everything is harder to do than it should be. With it, everything is easier, and your performance is actually better than your capability should make it. For that reason I often advise leaders to spend less time trying to fix problems and more trying to create momentum.

Production-level leaders understand momentum and use it to the organization's advantage. They also understand that there are three types of people when it comes to momentum:

Momentum Makers—Producers who make things happen.

Momentum Takers—People who go along for the ride.
Momentum Breakers—People who cause problems and hurt morale.

As a leader, you need to put the majority of your time and energy into the momentum makers and place them strategically in the organization so that they make the greatest impact. Enlist their aid to help lead the momentum takers as you motivate them. Meanwhile, have candid conversations with the momentum breakers. Give them a chance to change their attitude and become productive members of the team. However, if they fail to rise up to the challenge, move them off of the team. If that is impossible, then isolate them from the rest of the team to minimize the damage they can do.

If you build solid permissional relationships on top of a foundation of positional rights and add the results of productivity, you will gain momentum. And when you do, you'll find that your work comes to fruition more quickly.

6. Leadership Production Is the Foundation for Team Building

Who wants to leave a championship team? No one! Who wants to leave the cellar dweller? Everyone! People simply love being on a winning team. Winners attract people—some good, some bad, some average. The key to building a winning team is recognizing, selecting, and retaining the best people from the ones you attract. The good news is that if you reach Level 3, you know what productivity looks like because you live it. The bad news is that having talented people on the team doesn't automatically guarantee success. You can still lose with good players, but you cannot win without them. The difference comes from building them into a team, which I'll discuss later in the chapter. But remember this: if you aren't a proven producer, you won't attract and keep other proven producers. That's why you need to succeed on Level 3.

The Downside of Production

The Weight of Leadership Just Got Heavier

Like everything else in life, the Production level of leadership has its downsides as well as its upsides. With Level 3 leadership, achievement within the organization becomes easier. However, the leadership itself doesn't become easy. Here are the four main downsides I've discovered on Level 3.

1. Being Productive Can Make You Think You're a Leader When You're Not

All great leaders are productive. However, it is possible to be a producer and not a leader. Personal success does not always translate into team success. Leadership is defined by what a person does with and for others. It is established by making the team better and more productive. It's measured by what the entire group accomplishes, not by the individual efforts of the person in charge. Good leadership is never based on what someone does by and for himself.

I know many individual producers who have no desire or ability to lead others. Some don't have the people skills. Others don't have the desire to be responsible for others or take the time to help them become productive. Organizations all over the world make the mistake of putting high producers into leadership positions only to watch them fail to lead well. This mistake is often made because a prerequisite for being an effective leader is the ability to be effective yourself, but it is not the only qualification. Good leaders must establish themselves in their position on Level 1, gain people's permission on Level 2, be productive on Level 3, *and* possess the desire to take the entire team to a higher level.

2. Productive Leaders Feel a Heavy Weight of Responsibility for Results

If a football team doesn't win, the coach gets fired. If a corporation doesn't make profits, the CEO gets the ax. If a politician doesn't do a good job for his constituents, he doesn't get reelected. In any organization, the responsibility for results rests with the leaders. Productivity is measurable. Organizational growth is tangible. Profitability is quantifiable. Leaders who fail to produce are held accountable. Leaders who add to them are rewarded—and then asked to achieve even more the next time. High performance requires high commitment.

Many leaders who reach Level 3 tire of leading because of the weight of responsibility they feel. Most leaders experience days when they wish no one was watching their performance, looking to them for direction, or wanting them to make something happen. However, effective leaders understand that the cost of leadership is carrying the responsibility of their team's success on their shoulders. That is a weight every leader feels, starting on Level 3. You will have to decide whether you are willing to carry it.

3. Production Leadership Requires Making Difficult Decisions

Whenever you see a thriving organization, you can be sure that its leaders made some very tough decisions—and are continuing to make them. Success is an uphill journey. People don't coast their way to effective leadership. If you want to lead at a higher level, be ready to make difficult decisions. On Level 2, leaders often have to start making difficult people decisions. On Level 3, leaders continue to make those but also add difficult production decisions.

It has been my observation that when leaders are confronted with these difficult decisions on Level 3, many fail to make them. What they may not understand until it's too late is that failing to do so will eventually disqualify them from leading. Their leadership potential becomes stunted, and they cannot remain on Level 3.

I encourage you to persevere—even in moments when you feel the way Moses must have felt when the Red Sea parted and the people waited for him to take them forward, saying to himself, *Why must I always go first?* Going first may not always be easy or fun, but it is always a requirement of leaders. It paves the way for the people who follow and increases their chances of success in completing the journey.

4. Production Leadership Demands Continual Attention to Level 2

Becoming accountable for the productivity of the team does not mean that leaders can stop caring for the people they lead. Remember, just because you add a new level of leadership doesn't mean you leave the previous one behind. There is a real temptation for leaders on the Production level to neglect relationships in pursuit of achieving a good bottom-line result. However, if leaders do that for an extended period of time, they burn their relationships with their people, and they will eventually find themselves back on Level 1. Don't fall into that trap. Keep developing the relationships and caring for them as you produce results. Stay relationally connected to your people. Get out among them and spend time with them. Put connection time on your schedule, if needed. Do whatever it takes to keep from losing what you've gained on Level 2.

Best Behaviors on Level 3

How to Make the Most of Production in Leadership

Moving up through Level 3 based upon solid Level 2 relationships is no small feat for any person. Many people find themselves incapable of achieving it. If you have the opportunity to lead a team and get to Level 3 with them, here is what you need to do to make the most of it.

1. Understand How Your Personal Gifts Contribute to the Vision

One of the keys to the Production level of leadership is understanding how your gifts and abilities can be used productively, to further the vision of the organization. There is a strong relationship between giftedness and effectiveness as a leader on the Production level.

The more focused you are within your talents, the more rapid the rate of growth and the greater the increase in your overall potential to be a productive leader. Part of that is personal. In previous chapters I discussed the importance of knowing yourself and deciding on your personal leadership style. This is slightly different. If you are a leader, you must have a sense of vision for your leadership. And it must align, at least at this stage in your development, with the vision of the organization you serve.

One of the hallmarks of successful leadership is knowing where every person adds value. Take some time to define each team member's area of contribution (including your own), and figure out how they all work together to make the team most effective. But remember, if you want your team or department to be good at what they do, then you need to become good at what you do. Productivity has to start with the leader. Focus there first, and you will earn opportunities to help others improve and reach their potential.

2. Cast Vision for What Needs to Be Accomplished

Vision casting is an integral part of leading. Fuzzy communication leads to unclear direction, which produces sloppy execution. Productive leaders create a clear link between the vision of the organization and the everyday production of the team. They show how the short term impacts the long term. They are clear in their communication and continually point the way for their team.

A compelling vision is clear and well defined, expansive and challenging. It is aligned with the shared values of the team. It is focused primarily on the end, not the means. It fits the giftedness of the team. And when it is communicated and understood, it fills the room with energy!

Leaders give their teams the greatest possible chance for

success in achieving the vision when they do the following three things.

Help People Define the Success of the Vision

How can an organization be successful if the people in it don't know what the target is? Team members need leaders to describe the vision and define a success. Take time to carefully craft your communication, and deliver it creatively as often as possible.

Help People Commit to the Success of the Vision

The commitment of the team begins with the commitment of the leader. Teams don't win unless their leaders are determined to do everything they can to succeed, to dedicate their productivity to advancing the organization toward the vision. Through this leaders gain credibility and their people gain the confidence to follow suit.

Help People Experience Success

Few things inspire people as much as victory does. As individuals on the team get to experience small successes, it motivates them to keep going and reach for larger successes. If you want your people to be inspired to win, then reward and celebrate the small daily victories that they achieve. Make them part of your personal victory celebrations whenever possible, giving them as much of the credit as you can. Not only does that motivate people, but it also helps them to enjoy the journey.

3. Begin to Develop Your People into a Team

Production makes team building possible. That can be accomplished only by a leader who is willing to push forward and lead the way. Team building is one of my favorite aspects of leading people because a good team is always greater than the sum of its parts and is able to accomplish more than individuals working alone. Working as a team is also just plain fun! There's a lot to say about teamwork—more than I have space for here. But I want to give you some critical things to think about related to team building as you strive to become good at leading on Level 3. Here are four things a successful team leader needs to keep in mind.

Team Members Should Complement One Another

One of UCLA basketball coach John Wooden's most famous quotes is, "The one who scores a basket has ten hands." In other words, it takes all the players to help one player make a basket. And it takes a leader to help them figure out how to do it and lead them through the process.

Team Members Should Understand Their Mission

Good leaders never assume that their team members understand the mission. Don't take for granted that they know what you know or believe what you believe. Don't assume they understand how their talents and efforts are supposed to contribute to the mission of the team. Communicate it often.

Team Members Should Receive Feedback about Their Performance

People always want to know how they're doing. If they're not succeeding, most of the time they want to know how to make adjustments to improve and are willing to change if they are convinced it will help them win. Productive leaders take responsibility for walking team members through that process.

Team Members Should Work in an Environment Conducive to Growth and Inspiration

The leaders, more than anyone else on a team, set the tone in a department or for an organization. Their attitude is contagious. If they are positive, encouraging, and open to growth, so are their people. Acknowledge the influence you have and use it to everyone's best advantage.

Developing a group of people into a productive team is no easy task. It's a challenge to get everybody working together to achieve a common vision. But it is definitely worth the effort. Being part of a team of people doing something of high value is one of the most rewarding experiences in life. As a leader, you have a chance to help people experience it. Don't shrink from that great opportunity.

4. Prioritize the Things That Yield High Return

To be an effective Level 3 leader, you must learn to not only get a lot done but also to get a lot of the right things done.

That means understanding how to prioritize time, tasks, resources, and even people. The best companies channel their resources into only a few arenas—ones where they can be successful.

Staying in your areas of strength—where your efforts yield the highest return—and out of your areas of weakness is one of the keys to personal productivity. And if you can help others on your team to do the same, then you can be successful in leadership on Level 3.

For years I have relied on the Pareto principle as a guideline to help me decide what is worth focusing on and what isn't. The Pareto principle basically says that if you do the top 20 percent of your to-do list, it will yield an 80 percent return on your efforts.

To help me understand what my top 20 percent is, I ask myself three questions:

- What is required of me? (What I must do)
- What gives me the greatest return? (What I should do)
- What is most rewarding to me? (What I love to do)

If you are early in your career or new to leadership, your must-do list will probably be the largest. Your goal as you climb the levels of leadership is to shift your time and attention to the should-dos and love-to-dos. And if you lead well enough for long enough and build a great team, your must-, should-, and love-to-do should be the same things.

As you lead your team, try to help every person get to the place where they are doing their should-dos and love-to-dos. That is where they will be most effective. As a rule of thumb, try to hire, train, and position people in such a way that

80 percent of the time they work in their strength zone,

15 percent of the time they work in a learning zone,

5 percent of the time they work outside their strength zone, and

0 percent of the time they work in their weakness zone.

To facilitate that, you must really know your people, understand their strengths and weaknesses, and be willing to have candid conversations with them. If you've done your work on Level 2, then you should be ready, willing, and able to do those things.

5. Be Willing and Ready to Be a Change Agent

Progress always requires change. Change in an organization is always a leadership issue. It takes a leader to create positive change. And the best way to start working as a change agent is to do what you do when trying to build a relationship. You need to find common ground. Leaders who want to make changes are often tempted to point out differences between themselves and others and then try to convince others why change is needed. But that rarely works.

Instead, focus on similarities and build upon those. To get started, look for common ground in the following areas:

- **Vision**: If your vision and others' can line up, then everyone will see it clearly and have a strong desire to see it come to fruition. That means you can probably work well together.
- **Values**: It's difficult to travel with others very long if your values don't align. Find out what others stand for and try to meet where you share the same standards.
- **Relationships**: Great teams have people who are as committed to one another as they are to the vision. If you've done the work on Level 2, you should already share common ground in this area.
- **Attitude**: If you are going to get people to work together for positive change, their attitudes need to be positive and tenacious. If they're not, there will be trouble ahead.
- **Communication**: For change to occur, communication must be open, honest, and ongoing. Ignorance breeds speculation that leads to wrong assumptions, and that undermines change.

If you can find or create common ground in these five areas, you can move forward and introduce change. That doesn't necessarily mean that being a change agent will be easy. But I can guarantee that if you don't win in those five areas, change will be very difficult.

6. Never Lose Sight of the Fact That Results Are Your Goal

There's a big difference between Level 3 leaders and critics who simply theorize about productivity. Good leaders have an orientation toward results. They know that results always matter—regardless of how many obstacles they face, what the economy does, what kinds of problems their people experience, and so on. They fight for productivity and are held accountable no matter what. Even when they experience success! If they gain momentum, they don't back off and coast. They press on and increase the momentum so that they can accomplish even greater things. And they help their people do the same.

Beliefs That Help a Leader Move Up to Level 4

Leadership is an exciting journey. The most talented and dedicated leaders feel the pull to go higher. They hear a call to continually grow and help others do the same. Their beliefs give them the incentive to climb, but their behaviors are what actually take them to the next level.

If you want to go to that next level, then embrace the following ideas while still on Level 3.

1. Production Is Not Enough

What's better than excellence at your work and high productivity from your team? Developing people so that they can lead with you. Great leaders measure themselves by what they get done through others. That requires developing people in a leadership culture. That is the focus of leaders on Level 4. If you have reached Level 3 with your team members and you lead a productive team, congratulations. You've achieved more than most people ever do. But don't settle for Production. Seek the higher levels, where you can help change people's lives.

2. People Are an Organization's Most Appreciable Asset

Most of what an organization possesses goes down in value. Facilities deteriorate. Equipment becomes out of date. Supplies get used up. What asset has the greatest potential for actually going up in value? People! But only if they are valued, challenged, and developed by someone capable of investing in them and helping them grow. Otherwise, they are like money put on deposit without interest. Their potential is high, but they aren't actually growing.

People don't appreciate automatically or grow accidentally. Growth occurs only when it's intentional. If you want to go to the next level in your leadership, think beyond Production and start thinking in terms of how you can help the individuals on your team to improve themselves and tap into their potential.

3. Growing Leaders Is the Most Effective Way to Realize Vision

Companies get better when their people get better. That's why investing in people always gives a positive return to an organization. Everything rises and falls on leadership. The more leaders an organization has, the greater its horsepower. The better leaders an organization has, the greater its potential. You cannot overinvest in people. Every time you increase the leadership ability of a person in the organization, you increase the ability of the organization to fulfill its

vision. Everything gets better when good leaders are leading the organization and creating a positive, productive work
environment.

4. People Development Is the Greatest Fulfillment for a Leader

Few things in life are better than seeing people reach their
potential. One of the keys to developing leaders—at any
level—is seeing people not as they are or as others see them
but as they could be. Seeing what could be—and helping to
make it a reality—takes vision, imagination, skill, and commitment. If you help people become bigger and better on the
inside, eventually they will become greater on the outside.
People are like trees: give them what they need to grow on a
continual basis for long enough and they will grow from the
inside out. And they will bear fruit. If you invest in people,
they will never be the same again. And neither will you. It is
impossible to help others without helping yourself.

Level 4
PEOPLE DEVELOPMENT

*Helping Individual Leaders Grow Extends
Your Influence and Impact*

Successful leaders understand that if they want to improve, they have to be willing to keep growing and changing. Each move up the 5 Levels of Leadership requires a paradigm shift and a change in the way a person leads. To reach the upper levels of leadership, which create elite organizations, leaders must transition from producers to developers because people are any organization's most appreciable asset.

Good leaders on Level 4 invest their time, energy, money, and thinking into growing others as leaders. They look at every person and try to gauge his or her potential to grow and lead—regardless of the individual's title, position, age, or experience. Every person is a potential candidate for development. This practice of identifying and developing people compounds the positives of their organization, because bringing out the best in a person is often a catalyst for bringing out the best in the team. Developing one person for leadership and success lays the foundation for developing others for success.

A leader on the People Development level puts only 20 percent of his or her focus on personal productivity while putting 80 percent of it on developing and leading others. This can be a difficult shift for highly productive people who are used to getting their hands dirty, but it's a change that can revolutionize an organization and give it a much brighter future.

The Upside of People Development

*The Potential of the Organization
Just Got Greater*

When you become capable of leading people on Level 4, the upside of leadership becomes even stronger and the potential of the organization increases dramatically. Here are the primary positive benefits of leading on the People Development level:

1. People Development Sets You Apart from Most Leaders

Most leaders are looking for ways to grow their organizations. Where do they usually focus their attention? On Level 3. They work to increase production. That's the wrong focus. How do you grow a company? By growing the people in it. And if you really want to expand the organization and its potential, focus on growing the leaders.

In a competitive business world, the ability to develop people is often the difference maker between two organizations competing to succeed using similar resources. Former secretary of labor Robert Reich pointed out, "If employers fail to upgrade their workers, then they're trying to be competitive only with their capital. Anybody can replicate physical capital. But the one resource nobody can replicate is the dedication, the teamwork, the skills of a company's employees." Develop them, and you become a one-in-a-thousand leader.

2. People Development Assures That Growth Can Be Sustained

Achieving success isn't easy. Thousands of new businesses are launched every year only to fail a short time later. Those that make it discover that sustaining success isn't easy, either. Many companies said to have been "built to last" don't. Even some of the giants who seem invincible don't remain successful forever. What gives an organization the best chance for sustaining growth and success? Developing and training people. Only by helping your people reach their potential will your organization reach its potential.

Author Stephen Covey observed, "People and organizations don't grow much without delegation and completed staff work, because they are confined to the capacities of the boss and reflect both personal strengths and weaknesses." Don't allow yourself to become the lid on your organization. Give it the best chance for a bright future by developing other leaders.

3. People Development Empowers Others to Fulfill Their Leadership Responsibilities

People development is more than just teaching. It's transforming. It invites people into the process of leadership because many things can be learned only through experience. When established leaders focus on People Development and empower others to lead, everybody wins.

The first benefit comes to the people being led. When new leaders are developed, they become better at what they do and they help everyone who works with them to do the same. When these new leaders start building relationships with their people on Level 2, they treat them better and the working environment improves. When they master Level 3, they become more productive.

The second benefit comes to the organization. With the addition of more good leaders, the organization's current efforts improve. Every developed leader adds more horsepower to the organization. And expanding the leadership of the organization also gives it the ability to expand its territory and take on new initiatives.

The final benefit comes to the leaders who are doing the developing, because new leaders help to share the load. All leaders feel a weight of responsibility for leading. They understand that leaders are expected to produce no matter what. They feel a responsibility to the organization and their leaders to fulfill the vision. If there are stockholders, they feel responsible to them for making a profit. They feel responsible to the people they lead. They want to help them succeed. And they know that people's jobs are ultimately on the line.

As you develop people and they begin to share the load of leadership, it's important for you to give them the right expectations. Let them know that you're responsible to them, but not for them. By that I mean you will take responsibility for providing training, supplying tools, offering opportunities, and creating an environment conducive for their development. They must take responsibility for their growth through their choices, attitude, and commitment. If they don't, you will pay for their failure along with them, but that is a risk worth taking because the upside advantages if they succeed are so great. And when it does work and people seize the opportunity to grow and lead, it's fantastic.

4. People Development Empowers the Leader to Lead Larger

Many leaders don't want to share responsibility with others because they don't want to lose any of their power. But when you share leadership with others, it doesn't actually take away from you. Instead, it gives you time. As you develop people and empower them to lead, their territories expand and so does yours. But you are also freed up to do more important things, the most important of which include thinking, envisioning, and strategizing.

It's often difficult to hand over responsibility for a task to others, especially if you believe they won't do as good a job as you will. But that's no excuse. You cannot become an effective Level 4 leader unless you are willing to let go of some of your responsibilities. A good rule of thumb for transferring ownership of a leadership responsibility to someone else is the 80 percent rule. If someone on the team can do one of your tasks 80 percent as well as you do (or better), then give him or her responsibility for it. If you want to be an effective leader, you must move from perfectionist to pragmatist.

5. People Development Provides Great Personal Fulfillment

The greatest satisfaction in life comes when we forget ourselves and focus on others. And what's really wonderful is that when we add the giving that comes from developing people on Level 4 to the solid relationships we've developed on Level 2, the closeness and warmth that result can provide the richest experiences of our lives. We are often closest to people when we help them grow.

Rabbi Harold Kushner asserted, "The purpose of life is not to win. The purpose of life is to grow and to share. When you come to look back on all that you have done in life, you will get more satisfaction from the pleasures you have brought into other people's lives than you will from the times that you outdid and defeated them." That is great wisdom. Helping others grow and develop brings great joy, satisfaction, and energy to a leader. If you can achieve Level 4 as a leader, you will create a sense of community, where victories are celebrated, gratitude is evident, and loyalty is shared. Level 4 is the sweetest of all levels a leader can achieve.

The Downside of People Development

Leading on Level 4 Requires High Levels of Maturity and Skill

There is a reason that many leaders don't develop people. It's not easy! And there's no guarantee that it will work out. Every leader has horror stories of investment in others that turned out badly. You pour yourself into some people and nothing happens. Some people take without giving anything in return. Others make an effort but fall far short of your expectations. And sometimes you give your best to someone, he turns out to be an absolute star, and then he leaves and becomes part of another organization! What can be worse than that? Well, how about not training him and having him stay? If you think about it, you have only one great choice as a leader if you want to lead to the full extent of your potential: you need to invest in your people.

People development requires a very high maturity level. It also requires a very high level of skill. That can create problems for some leaders, and it prevents many from following through with it. Here are the primary causes of breakdowns on Level 4.

1. Self-Centeredness Can Cause Leaders to Neglect People Development

Maturity is the ability to think beyond yourself, see things from the perspective of others, and place their needs above your own. Selfishness prevents some people from reaching that level of maturity. If you want to lead on Level 4, you need to focus 80 percent of your attention on others and helping them to grow, learn, and achieve. If your focus is always on yourself and what you want, then people become an obstacle to your goals. Their needs are seen as interfering with your goals. And you spend most of your time disappointed with others because they aren't on your agenda and are forever letting you down. You shouldn't go into people development selfishly. Don't do it because people cause trouble and you want them to change. You should go into it because people are worth it, and you're willing to take the trouble to help them.

If you want to move up to Level 4 leadership, get over your selfishness, get outside of yourself, and adopt the attitude of speaker and master salesman Zig Ziglar, who said, "If you will help others get what they want, they will help you get what you want."

2. Insecurity Can Make Leaders Feel Threatened by People Development

Insecure leaders continually sabotage themselves and others. Because they worry about their position and standing, fearing that someone will take their place, they have a hard time investing in other people. Leaders who don't deal with their insecurities and overcome them rarely reach Level 4 as leaders. If you suspect that your insecurities may prevent you from moving up to the People Development level of leadership, then be prepared to do some work in the following three areas.

Ego

Leaders who are honest with themselves know that they don't have all the answers. They recognize that success comes when people work together, each person playing his or her part. Because of this, they don't try to answer every question themselves. They don't try to make every decision. They see winning as a collaborative effort. And their goal isn't to make others think more highly of them. It's to get their people to think more highly of themselves.

How can you tell if your ego might be getting in the way of your ability to move up to Level 4? Consider what happens when you meet with your team.

- Do your team members share their thoughts and ideas freely?
- Are the best ideas coming from others?
- If you often contribute ideas, does the discussion quickly move from your idea to the best idea—and you're happy about it?

Now consider what happens when your team performs.

- When your team succeeds, do the other team members get the majority of the credit?
- Is there a shared sense of pride in the work that's being done?
- When things go wrong, do you personally accept the greatest share of the blame?

If you can honestly answer yes to these questions, ego may not be a problem. If you answered no to many of those questions, beware. You may need to deal with your ego. Positive working environments led by secure leaders allow team members to get the credit. Level 4 leaders experience genuine joy in the success of others. When others shine, so do they.

Control

Many insecure workers try to avoid making mistakes by doing as little as possible or by trying to keep a low profile. Insecure leaders, on the other hand, often deal with the issue by relying on control. They think if they micromanage their people, they can keep them from making mistakes. But progress comes only from taking risks and making mistakes. Good leaders forge ahead, break ground, and make mistakes.

Since you can't prevent mistakes, why not adopt an attitude

in which you and your team learn from them? That's the only way anyone can really profit from mistakes anyway. Don't try to put people in a box. Try to help them make the most of their fumbles, flops, and failures. As Jack Welch, the former CEO of General Electric, said, "A leader's role is not to control people or stay on top of things, but rather to guide, energize, and excite." That's what Level 4 leaders do.

Trust

Insecure leaders don't place their trust in others, nor do they engender trust from others. As a result, they don't invest in others. And they don't become Level 4 leaders. As a leader, you should never take trust for granted. Only when you lose it do you really understand the value of it. If you want to become a People Development leader, you must give others your trust and earn their trust in return. There is no other way to succeed on Level 4.

3. Shortsightedness Can Keep Leaders from Seeing the Need for People Development

How many times have you considered giving someone something to do and instead thought, *It's easier to just do it myself*? Doing work yourself is always faster and easier than developing other people so that they can do it. But that's short-term thinking! To become a developer of people, you have to be willing to adopt a long-term mind-set. If you pay the price on the front end, the return is great on the back end. On Level 4, the question isn't, what can you do? The question is, whom can you develop? Investing in people takes a lot of time and energy.

Shortsightedness, like selfishness and insecurity, is another sign of immaturity in a leader. People Development requires big-picture thinking. It takes patience. Helping another person to become a competent leader almost always takes longer than you think and is more difficult than you expect. You must do it anyway. Otherwise you limit the potential for yourself, your people, and your organization.

4. Lack of Commitment Can Keep Leaders from Doing the Hard Work of People Development

Anyone who can relate well with people, produce personally, and communicate a vision is capable of attracting a following. However, attracting, developing, and leading other leaders is much more difficult. And most leaders are not willing to put forth the tremendous effort it takes and make the sacrifices necessary to do it.

For some, the idea of giving themselves away by developing and empowering others to lead is very counterintuitive. Those people fear it will lessen them. But many others get it. They do it. And they see the incredible impact People Development can make. It transforms organizations and even impacts cultures. But it takes a high level of security and skill to do. And it requires a high degree of commitment.

Best Behaviors on Level 4

How to Develop People

Only leaders can develop other people to become leaders. A well-intentioned person with no leadership knowledge and experience cannot train another person to lead. Theorists who study leadership without practicing it cannot equip someone to lead, any more than a cookbook reader who has no experience in the kitchen would be able to teach someone how to cook. Nobody really understands leadership until he or she does it. Put another way...

- It Takes a Leader to KNOW a Leader (Recruiting and Positioning)
- It Takes a Leader to SHOW a Leader (Modeling and Equipping)
- It Takes a Leader to GROW a Leader (Developing, Empowering, and Measuring)

In light of that truth, my goal in this section on People Development is to give you a clear path to follow as you seek to develop other people to lead. If you want to make the most of People Development and raise up others to lead, then follow these guidelines.

1. Recruiting—Find the Best People Possible

Recruiting is the first and most important task in developing people and creating winning organizations. You can't develop people without potential—no matter how hard you work at it. So the people you recruit must possess natural ability in the area where they are to be developed, exhibit the desire to grow, and be a good fit for the organization.

The key to success in recruiting is a clear picture of who you are looking for. Recruiting a nonleader to be developed in leadership is like asking a horse to climb a tree. It just isn't going to happen. If you want a potential tree climber, find a squirrel. If you want a potential leader, find someone with the traits of a good leader.

When I go looking for potential leaders, I use what I call the Four *C*s.

Chemistry

If you don't like the person, you will not be an effective mentor to him or her. It's very difficult to spend time with people, be open with them, and invest in them if you don't like them and want to be around them.

If you are seriously considering recruiting or promoting someone, ask members of your team to spend time with that individual, preferably in a social setting. After they've been around the person, find out if your team likes and would enjoy working with him or her. If not, there may not be a good fit.

Character

Good character makes trust possible. Trust makes strong relationships possible. Strong relationships make mentoring possible. You won't be able to develop someone whose character you do not trust.

Character is what closes the gap between knowing and doing. It aligns intentions and action. That consistency is appealing, and it is also essential to good, credible leadership. Jim Rohn observed, "Good people are found, not changed." If you go into a mentoring relationship expecting to change a person's character, you're liable to be disappointed.

Capacity

If you want to develop people and help them become good leaders, you must not ask for what they wish they could give, only for what they have the potential to give. As you look at potential leaders, try to assess their capacity in the following areas:

- **Stress Management**—their ability to withstand and overcome pressure, failure, deadlines, and obstacles
- **Skill**—their ability to get specific tasks done

- **Thinking**—their ability to be creative, develop strategy, solve problems, and adapt
- **Leadership**—their ability to gather followers and build a team
- **Attitude**—their ability to remain positive and tenacious amid negative circumstances

As a leader, your goal should be to identify the capacities of potential leaders, recognize what they think their capacities are, and motivate, challenge, and equip them in such a way that they close the gap between the two.

Contribution

Some people possess an X factor. They are winners. They contribute beyond their job responsibilities, and they lift the performance of everyone on their team. When you discover people with these characteristics, recruit them. They are a joy to develop, and whatever you put into them returns to you many times over.

Most leaders spend their time and energy on the wrong people: the bottom 20 percent. The individuals who usually take up most of a leader's time are the troublemakers, the complainers, and those who are struggling. These people often have the least potential to lead others and take the organization forward. Level 4 leaders focus their best time and energy on the top 20 percent, the people who don't need attention but would most profit from it.

2. Positioning—Placing the Right People in the Right Position

It's not enough just to recruit good team members. A leader must understand how those people best fit on the team and put them there. To do that, he must have a clear picture of each person's strengths and weakness and understand how they fit the needs of the team.

Some leaders take a counseling approach to developing people. By that I mean that they focus on what the person is doing poorly or wrong, and they focus their attention on helping them make corrections in those areas. If you want to develop people, though, you must help them discover and build upon their strengths. That's where people have the most potential to grow. Helping to develop their strengths is the only way to help leaders become world-class.

3. Modeling—Showing Others How to Lead

Few things are worse than the teacher who is unteachable. As a leader, you will reproduce what you are. For example, if you remain teachable, your people will remain teachable. If your mind is closed, the minds of the people you mentor will probably be closed. You set the tone for those who follow you.

One of the secrets of developing leaders on Level 4 is to have the people you are mentoring beside you as often as possible so that they can learn how you think and act in a variety of situations. Here are the things I believe I must display, or model, with integrity in order to help people to develop on Level 4:

Authenticity—This is the foundation for developing people.
Servanthood—This is the soul for developing people.
Growth—This is the measurement for developing people.
Excellence—This is the standard for developing people.
Passion—This is the fuel for developing people.
Success—This is the purpose for developing people.

Your goal at first is for them to observe as you model leadership. But as quickly as you can, move on to the next phase of development.

4. Equipping—Helping Others Do Their Jobs Well

It's not enough to simply tell people what they need to do. That's not developing their potential. Instead, a leader must help them to do their jobs and do them well. The best method I've ever found is a five-step equipping process. Here's how it works:

Step 1—I do it (competence).
Step 2—I do it and you are with me (demonstration).
Step 3—You do it and I am with you (coaching).
Step 4—You do it (empowerment).
Step 5—You do it and someone is with you (reproduction).

If you adopt this method, not only will you equip leaders, you will begin teaching them how to equip others, which sets them up to become Level 4 leaders themselves.

5. Developing—Teaching Them to Do Life Well

If the only thing you're helping a new leader learn is how to get ahead in the workplace, you're not truly developing that person to succeed, because there's a lot more to life than work and career. The Center for Creative Leadership has observed that three key elements drive leadership development in others.

Assessment

As a Level 4 leader, you should be continually on the lookout for holes in the life skills of someone you are leading and developing. Ask yourself:

Where does this person seem to be failing?

Where are this person's blind spots?

What does my intuition tell me is "off" in this person's thinking?

Why isn't this person reaching his or her potential?

Who might be leading this person in a wrong direction?

When does this person do well?

When does this person stumble?

What telltale clues can I find that give me insight into where this person needs help?

Where is this person's sweet spot?

A good Level 4 leader is always on the lookout for a person's weaknesses and wrong thinking—not to exploit that person, but to strengthen and help him or her succeed.

Challenge

If you've done your work on Level 2 to build a strong relationship with the people on your team, and you've proven yourself on Level 3 by demonstrating success and modeling productivity, there is a very good chance that people on your team will buy into your leadership and accept a challenge from you to improve. To present that challenge, ask the people you lead to do the following:

- Read books related to their areas of strength.
- Attend conferences that will inspire them.
- Take on new and challenging tasks in their sweet spot.
- Practice difficult disciplines that slowly build character.
- Meet with you on a regular basis for mentoring.

The idea is to challenge them in the areas of their lives where you see that they need improvement. Just be sure to gain their permission to do it before starting the process.

Support

Nobody gets ahead in life without the help and support of other people. One of the great privileges of leading on the People Development level is helping new leaders navigate through life's difficulties.

It's difficult for people to make the most of their leadership potential when the rest of their lives is a wreck. Good life skills help a person to create a strong foundation upon which to build a family, career, and spiritual life. I admit that I get the greatest joy from seeing people reach their leadership potential, but it is also very satisfying to know that I've helped someone to enjoy life and live it well.

6. Empowering—Enabling People to Succeed

Empowerment means helping people to see what they can do without your help, and releasing them to do it. As you release tasks to the leaders you're developing, you need to trust them, believe in them, and hold them accountable. Trust creates a bond between you and them. When I trust the people I empower, I put a little piece of myself into their hands. When they respond in kind, the shared vulnerability creates a bond that deepens the relationship.

When you believe in people, you motivate them. And the belief must be genuine. Pretending you believe provides no passion for empowerment. Nor can you borrow the belief from someone else, because it will have no power. You must draw upon the experiences you have with people and the growth that they have already exhibited. Besides helping them, it will also help you. If you don't believe in them, you won't be able to let go and release them to achieve.

When you hold people accountable, you increase their chances for positive results. Why? Because everyone finds focus in goals. They work better toward deadlines. And they usually rise to the level of a leader's expectations. Without accountability, people drift. With it, they achieve results.

7. Measuring—Evaluating Those Whom You Develop to Maximize Their Efforts

Many people look at winning sports teams and attribute the team's success to how knowledgeable the coach is. But games aren't won according to what the coach knows. Games are won according to what the coach's players have learned. How can you measure that as a leader? By judging how independently your team members are able to function.

The Center for Organizational Leadership in Cincinnati, Ohio, suggests that leaders should employ different degrees of empowerment, based on how independently a team member can work. Here are the six they recognize, from least independent to most independent:

1. Look into it. Report. I'll decide what to do.
2. Look into it. Report alternatives with pros and cons and your recommendation.
3. Look into it. Let me know what you intend to do, but don't do it unless I say yes.
4. Look into it. Let me know what you intend to do and do it unless I say no.
5. Take action. Let me know what you did.
6. Take action. No further contact required.

As you work in People Development with team members, you can measure where they are based on how they typically function according to those six benchmarks. Obviously, your goal is to help them become leaders who can take action without needing your input. When the leaders you develop reach that benchmark, then they—and you—are ready to lead them at the highest level of leadership, Level 5.

Beliefs That Help a Leader Move Up to Level 5

If you have managed to move up to Level 4, you are leading at a very high level, higher than 90 percent of all other leaders. But there is still one level higher that may be within your reach. Fewer than 1 percent of all leaders achieve it. To prepare yourself to attempt that final climb and give yourself the best chance of making it to the top, you must first embrace the following beliefs.

1. The Highest Goal of Leadership Is to Develop Leaders, Not Gain Followers or Do Work

Getting work done can be important and rewarding. And leading others and having them help you achieve a vision can be wonderful. But developing others is even more wonderful. And it should be your goal as a leader.

Improvement of individual leaders' lives is the highest goal of leadership development. When you help other people become leaders, you change their lives. You change the way they see the world. You change their capacity. You increase their potential. You change the way they interact with others. If they become good leaders, you help them improve not only their lives but also the lives of everyone they touch. I believe that is how you change the world for the better.

I described in Level 3 how the Pareto principle can be used to increase productivity. That same principle can be used when developing leaders. As a Level 4 leader, you should focus 80 percent of your attention on developing the best 20 percent of the leaders you have. That focus will bring you the highest return. A handful of leaders will give an organization a far greater return than hundreds of followers.

Focusing your development on the top 20 percent also sets you up for success on Level 5 because the leaders with the most potential, and who give you the highest rate of return on your investment, also have the greatest likelihood of turning around and raising up other leaders, which is the emphasis on Level 5.

2. To Develop Leaders, You Must Create a Leadership Culture

Even if you place great emphasis on developing leaders and practice the 80–20 rule, you will not be able to move up to Level 5 unless you also create a leadership culture. If you want to start creating a culture that cultivates Level 5 leaders, then do the following:

Champion Leadership—Define and model good leadership.

Teach Leadership—Train leaders on a regular, frequent, consistent basis.

Practice Leadership—Help emerging leaders to plan and execute, fail and succeed.

Coach Leadership—Review new leaders' performance and correct their errors.

Reward Leadership—Reward good leadership with pay, resources, and recognition.

If you make the purpose of your organization to champion, teach, practice, coach, and reward leadership, then people will want to become good leaders. They will strive to help others become good leaders. And the potential of the organization to fulfill its vision will explode.

3. Developing Leaders Is a Life Commitment, Not a Job Commitment

Level 4 leaders develop people. Level 5 leaders consistently develop leaders over a lifetime, and the leaders they raise up also develop leaders. It becomes a lifestyle they practice everywhere and at all times, not a program they implement or a task they occasionally practice. Mentoring is a mantle that they wear willingly, and they strive to add value to others. They value it because they have transitioned from chasing a position of success to pursuing a role of significance.

We live in a very needy world. If you often ask yourself, *How do we meet so many needs?* then please realize that the greatest needs will never be met until we equip leaders who can work to meet those needs. That is one of the reasons I train leaders. I believe it is a cause worthy of a lifetime commitment. I hope you will accept the challenge to develop people and raise up leaders. If you do, you won't regret it.

Level 5
THE PINNACLE

*The Highest Leadership Accomplishment Is
Developing Other Leaders to Level 4*

Rare is the leader who reaches Level 5—the Pinnacle. Not only is leadership at this level a culmination of leading well on the other four levels, it also requires both a high degree of skill and some amount of natural leadership ability. It takes a lot to be able to develop other leaders so that they reach Level 4; that's what Level 5 leaders do. The individuals who reach Level 5 lead so well for so long that they create a legacy of leadership in the organization they serve.

Pinnacle leaders stand out from everyone else. They are a cut above, and they seem to bring success with them wherever they go. Leadership at this high level lifts the entire organization and creates an environment that benefits everyone in it, contributing to their success. Level 5 leaders often possess an influence that transcends the organizations and the industries they work in.

Most leaders who reach the Pinnacle do so later in their careers. But the Pinnacle level is not a resting place from which leaders should stop and view their success. It is a reproducing place from which they can make the greatest impact of their lives. That's why leaders who reach the Pinnacle should make the most of it while they can. With gratitude and humility, they should lift up as many leaders as they can, tackle as many great challenges as possible, and extend their influence to make a positive difference beyond their own organizations and industries.

The Upside of the Pinnacle

Your Influence Has Expanded beyond Your Reach and Your Time

When writing about Level 1, I told you that as you climbed the 5 Levels of Leadership, the upsides would continue to increase while the downsides would decrease. However, Level 5 doesn't fit that pattern. On the Pinnacle, I see only three major upsides. But though they are few, each carries a tremendous weight and huge impact.

1. Pinnacle Leadership Creates a Level 5 Organization

Many organizations seem to struggle to maintain their existence. Others work hard to inch their way toward growth or increased profitability. Meanwhile, a few organizations rise above the rest and seem to function at an extraordinarily high level. What's their secret? Leadership. Great organizations have great leaders, and the best organizations, which function at the highest capacity—Level 5 organizations—become what they are because they are led by Level 5 leaders.

Because Level 5 leaders empower many people to lead

larger, they lift the leadership lid for everyone in the organization. Because they produce lots of leaders and continue to do so over the long haul of their careers, their organizations develop an abundance mind-set. People in the organization receive lots of opportunities, and they expect to continue getting them. With the development of each leader and the pursuit of every opportunity, the organization continues to get stronger. And in time, leadership becomes part of their DNA. And even when one leader steps down or retires, there are many leaders ready and able to take their place because Level 5 organizations have a pipeline of leaders being produced.

Because Level 5 leaders have worked their way up through each level to arrive at the Pinnacle position, they understand and practice leadership at a high level. They have experienced a transformation of sorts with each transition from one level to another, and as a result they have insight that helps them to recognize where other leaders are in the process and to help those leaders navigate the various changes required to move up to the next level.

2. Pinnacle Leadership Creates a Legacy within the Organization

Level 5 leaders want to do more than just run an organization well. They want to do more than succeed. They want to create a legacy. If you reach the Pinnacle level, you have an opportunity to make an impact beyond your tenure and possibly beyond your own lifetime. You do that by developing a generation of leaders who will develop the next generation of leaders.

Level 5 leaders are measured by the caliber of leaders they develop, not the caliber of their own leadership. Their approach to leadership changes accordingly. In Level 5 organizations, when the top leader steps down, there are usually many leaders ready to rise up and take the reins. And the organization experiences a continuity unfamiliar to organizations with lesser leaders.

3. Pinnacle Leadership Provides an Extended Platform for Leading

In America, we believe everyone has the right to speak. But even in a free society, you have to earn the right to be heard. Level 5 leaders have paid their dues and earned that right. And because they lead well and develop others to do likewise, their influence extends beyond their reach. People outside of their direct sphere of influence hear about them and seek them out for advice. Level 5 leaders are able to cross lines out of their industry or area of expertise to speak with authority. People respect them for who they are and what they represent. That gives them a greater platform and extended influence. They often have a chance to make a broader impact on society or to advance the cause of leadership, redefine it, and pour themselves into the next generation of leaders.

With this extended influence comes a responsibility to steward it with integrity. Level 5 leaders understand that the highest position of leadership is not a place to be served by others but to serve others. It is not a place to receive, but a place to give.

The Downside of the Pinnacle

You May Start to Believe It's All about You

Each level of leadership has its downside. This level is no exception. But here's the good news: fewer leaders become victims of the downside at the Pinnacle level than at any other. Why? Because it's difficult to reach the Pinnacle without a great measure of maturity. Every lesson leaders learn at the previous levels becomes a curb that helps to keep them from getting off course. However, here is the bad news. Those who are susceptible to the downside on the Pinnacle fall dramatically. They can derail everything they've worked for up to this point.

Here are the three negative things you need to look out for if you reach the Pinnacle.

1. Being on the Pinnacle Can Make You Think You've Arrived

It's ironic, but one of the greatest dangers for Pinnacle leaders at the top is similar to a danger for Position leaders at the bottom: thinking they've arrived. If you came into leadership with a destination mind-set, and you carried it with you as you've moved your way up through the 5 Levels of Leadership, you may think that the Pinnacle is a place to rest, smell the roses, and make the most of your privileges. If that's your mind-set, beware!

Leaders who have reached the top of their profession or the top of their organization cannot take anything for granted. No matter how good they've been in the past, they still need to strategize, weigh decisions, plan, and execute at a high level. Momentum can overcome a lot of problems, but even great momentum cannot continually compensate for negligence, arrogance, or stupidity.

Pinnacle leaders also should not treat the organization as their personal property—even if it is their property. Every organization for which people work is a trust. If you're the leader, you cannot make decisions with only you and your personal interests in mind. To whomever much is given, much will be required.

People who reach the top of their field are always in danger of thinking they have nothing left to learn. If that happens to you, it's the beginning of the end. To be effective, leaders must always be learners. You can never arrive—you can only strive to get better. That is the mind-set you must bring to every day of your leadership. If you're through learning, you're through.

The best way to develop and maintain a teachable attitude is to do three things:

1. Write a credo for learning that you will follow every day; it should describe the attitude and actions you will embrace to remain teachable.

2. Find one or more people who are ahead of you in leadership that you can meet with periodically to learn from.

3. Dedicate yourself to a hobby, task, or physical activity outside of your expertise to keep you challenged, teachable, and humble.

2. Being on the Pinnacle Can Lead You to Believe Your Own Press

Few things are more ridiculous than leaders who take themselves too seriously and begin to believe they are God's gift to others. Yet it happens continually. History is filled with stories of people who got carried away with their power and position.

Any time a leader begins to believe his own press, he's in trouble. When people excel to a high level in their profession, a type of mythology grows up around them. They become larger than life in other people's minds. A lot of the time it's hype. Level 5 leaders are rarely as good as people give them credit for. And no leaders—no matter how long or how well they've led—are above the laws of leadership. The laws are like gravity. They apply to you whether or not you believe in them.

If you become a Level 5 leader, never forget that, like everyone else, you started at the bottom, as a positional leader. You had to work to build relationships. You had to prove your productivity. And investing in the lives of others came about only with effort. Be confident, but also be humble. If you've become successful, it's only because a lot of other people helped you all along the way.

3. Being on the Pinnacle Can Make You Lose Focus

When leaders reach Level 5, the number of opportunities they receive becomes extraordinary. Everyone wants to hear what such leaders have to say. But many of these opportunities are really little more than distractions. They won't help the leader's organization or cause.

If leaders who reach the Pinnacle want to make the most of their time there, they must remain focused on their vision and purpose and continue leading at the highest level. No matter where you are in your leadership journey, never forget that what got you to where you are won't get you to the next level. Each step forward requires focus and a willingness to keep learning, adapting, strategizing, and working. You don't stay on top without focus, humility, and hard work.

Best Behaviors on Level 5

How to Use the Pinnacle as a Platform to Do Something Greater Than Yourself

Leadership should always be about others, not about the leader. That's true at every level, and it's especially important on Level 5, because having people follow out of deep respect is the height of leadership. Pinnacle leaders have a lot of horsepower, and they need to make good use of it while they're on top to do more than help themselves. Here are my suggestions.

1. Make Room for Others at the Top

Most leaders make it their goal to cultivate followers. But gathering followers doesn't create room for other leaders. As a Pinnacle leader, you must create that room and do so by developing leaders. If you do that continually and promote good leaders whenever you can, you create a cycle of positive change in the organization that creates room for leaders.

That may seem counterintuitive. Wouldn't having more leaders create less room? No. And here's why: when you develop a leader who develops other leaders, you create more room at the top because you increase the size and power of the entire organization. Every time you develop good leaders and help find a place for them to lead and make an impact, they gather more good people to them. As a result, the organization grows (along with its potential) and it needs more good leaders. This process creates a cycle of expansion and a kind of momentum toward the top for other leaders, which helps to propel the organization forward.

Take a look at your organizational chart. Are there places available for talented leaders who desire to move up? Take a look at the leaders who are near the top of the chart. Of what caliber are they? How long have they been with the organization? How long are they likely to stay? Are they so firmly entrenched that the talented leaders below them in the organization have little hope of advancing? If there are no openings and the leaders you have aren't going anywhere, then there is no room at the top for other potential leaders. How can you create some? What new challenges can you give your existing top leaders to open up their current positions to others? What kinds of expansion or types of initiatives could your organization tackle that would require additional leaders?

If you don't create room at the top for developing leaders, you will waste much of your potential horsepower, and you will eventually start to lose your up-and-coming talent.

2. Continually Mentor Potential Level 5 Leaders

I've been teaching and writing on the subject of leadership for three and a half decades, and in that time I've had the privilege of working with a lot of organizations. Each of them has been unique, with questions, needs, and conditions unlike any other. However, all of them have had one thing in common. They needed more and better leaders! Not once has anyone in an organization said, "We have too many leaders. And the ones we have are better than we want. Can you help us get rid of some?"

No matter what your leadership potential may be, you should strive to work your way up to Level 4 so that you can invest in others. But if you reach Level 5, you have a much greater responsibility. Leaders with high potential will only follow leaders who are ahead of them—in ability, experience, or both. For that reason, Pinnacle leaders cannot delegate the leadership development process of potential leaders to others who are less talented than those being mentored. It simply doesn't work. If there are potential Level 4 or Level 5 leaders in your organization and you're a Level 5 leader, you must dedicate the time and effort to mentoring them. Otherwise they will go elsewhere to find a Level 5 leader who is willing to do it. The best potential leaders will not remain in the organization unless you go to them where they are, extend your hand, and help them to climb up to your level.

3. Create an Inner Circle That Will Keep You Grounded

The Law of the Inner Circle says that those closest to leaders determine their potential. When leaders reach Level 4, their inner circle makes them better. Inner circle members help leaders take their organization to a higher level. That's still true on Level 5, but the inner circle must also fulfill another function: it must keep the leader grounded. A good inner circle can help leaders on the Pinnacle level to avoid the pitfall of believing their own press, which I mentioned earlier.

Inner circle members allow leaders to be themselves, but will also tell them the truth about themselves. Here is what I ask my inner circle to do:

- Love me unconditionally.
- Represent me according to my values.
- Watch my back.
- Complement my weaknesses.
- Continue to grow.
- Fulfill their responsibilities with excellence.
- Be honest with me.
- Tell me what I need to hear, not what I want to hear.
- Help carry the weight, not be an extra weight.
- Work together as a team.
- Add value to me.
- Enjoy the journey with me.

The people in my inner circle give me these things, and in return I give them my loyalty, love, and protection; I reward them financially; I develop them in leadership; I give them opportunities; and I share my blessings.

Having a strong inner circle will keep the journey enjoyable, prevent loneliness, and keep leaders from developing hubris. And here's the good news. The people in your inner circle can become your favorite people—like family.

4. Do Things for the Organization That Only Level 5 Leaders Can Do

Being on Level 5 allows a leader to see and do things that cannot be done from any other place in leadership. Some of those things are obvious. If you're the top leader in your organization, you need to guide it. You need to be a good model to everyone in the organization by valuing people, continuing to grow, practicing the golden rule, being authentic, exhibiting good values, and living out the right priorities.

Other things may be less obvious and very specific to your situation and organization. You may be able to create a groundbreaking product or service. You may be able to champion a value or cause that no one else could as effectively. You may be able to help people improve their lives. You may be able to impact your community in a unique way. You may have relationships with people who can help you to do something important. All the work you've done and all the influence you've gained over the years just might be in your hands so that you can do something bigger with it. You have to keep your eyes, ears, and heart open to the possibilities. The success you have hasn't been given to you for only yourself. Level 5 leaders have a platform from which they can lead and persuade. Whenever possible, use it to pass on those things that have helped you. Leadership is influence. Leverage it to add value to others.

5. Plan for Your Succession

Leaving a successor is the last great gift a leader can give an organization. Leadership transition difficulties are far too common, and, like the passing of the baton in a relay race, a leadership transition must be planned and executed well. Success is dependent upon the leader with the baton handing it off to the next leader when both of them are running at maximum speed. True leaders put ego aside and strive to create successors who go beyond them. And they plan to hand off the baton of leadership when they are still running at their peak. If a leader has already begun to slow down, the baton is being handed off too late. No leader should hurt the organization's momentum by staying too long just for his or her own gratification. The number one problem in organizations led by Level 5 leaders is that they stay too long. So if you're a Level 5 leader who runs an organization, plan your succession and leave before you feel you have to.

6. Leave a Positive Legacy

One of the keys to arriving at the end of our lives without regret is doing the work of creating a lasting legacy. If you are a Level 5 leader, I want to encourage you to use the influence you have now to create a better world. How? First, recognize that what you do daily, over time, becomes your legacy. Whether it's spending quality time with your family every day, saving money and investing every month, or speaking kind and encouraging words to others each day—these actions result in a legacy of positive impact.

Second, decide now what you want your legacy to be. How do you want to be remembered? What would you like people to say about you at your funeral? Do you have a vision for the positive impact you want to leave behind you? Do you know what you can invest in potential leaders who will want to help you build it?

Finally, understand that a legacy is the sum of your whole life, not just snippets. If you have failed, that's okay. Has your life taken a path that is less than ideal? Put it behind you. Set off in the right direction and begin to change the way you live starting today. Fulfill your mission and vision for your life. Do it now before it is too late to change.

Don't let yourself get to the final days of your life wondering what could have been. Decide today what your life will be, and then take action each and every day to live your dreams and leave your legacy!

Help Others Move Up to
Levels 4 and 5

*Create Crucible Moments for the Leaders
You Develop*

At this point in previous sections of the book, I discussed the beliefs that will help you to move up to the next level of leadership. However, when you're on the Pinnacle level, there is no higher place in leadership. So in this section I am going teach you how to help others to move up to the higher levels of leadership. Besides, once you reach Level 5, your focus shouldn't be on advancing yourself; it should be on helping others move up as high as they can go.

What is the secret of learning to lead? Leading. That's like saying that you learn to drive a car by driving a car. Or that you learn to cook by cooking. A little experience goes a lot further than a lot of theory. As a mentor, you can give the inexperienced leaders leadership experiences that make them better. As an experienced leader, you can identify potential leaders, you can figure out what kinds of experiences they need, and you can help to provide them in a controlled environment where their failures and fumbles won't completely take them out of the game of leadership. I call these experiences crucible moments. The key incidents in your life—the crucible moments—have shaped you. They've created breakthroughs for you. And the leadership experiences you've had—both good and bad—have made you the leader you are today. The same will be true for those you lead and develop.

If you want to make the most of your influence on Level 5, then you need to create crucible moments that will enable your best leaders to reach their leadership potential. Here's how I suggest you go about doing it.

1. Identify and Create the Crucial Lessons Leaders Must Learn

Begin by identifying the essential qualities and skills any good leader must possess. This will be your blueprint for introducing key experiences and testing potential leaders as they become ready. Here is a list I developed after my fortieth birthday, when I realized I needed to dedicate myself to developing my inner circle of leaders:

Integrity
Problem-Solving
Vision
Communication
Influence
Creativity

Passion
Teamwork
Servanthood
Attitude
Confidence
Self-Discipline

Once I had settled on the list, I began to look for opportunities to put leaders in situations where they could learn experience-based lessons in those areas. For example, whenever there was a problem in the organization, I didn't solve it myself. Instead, I sent one of the leaders I was developing to try to figure it out. Afterward, we'd discuss how he or she solved the problem and what he or she learned. To help their communication, when leaders were ready, I'd give them an opportunity to speak: to various groups, to the organization's leaders, or to the entire organization. Afterward we'd talk about what went wrong and what went right, and what they could do the next time to improve. If I wanted to help them develop their influence and improve their teamwork, I'd ask them to recruit a team of volunteers for an event or a program and work with that team to follow through. You get the idea. When you lead an organization, you can't be focused on just fulfilling the vision or getting work done. Every challenge, problem, opportunity, or initiative is a chance for you to pair potential leaders to a leadership development experience that will change who they are. Try to think in those terms every day.

2. Look for Unexpected Crucible Moments Leaders Can Learn From

People don't learn things just because we want them to. Level 5 leaders understand that teachable moments often come as the result of "levers" in their lives. Change occurs in people's lives when they . . .

Hurt enough that they have to (Pain and Adversity),
Learn enough that they want to (Education and Experience), or
Receive enough that they are able to (Support and Equipping).

Wise leaders look for moments that fall into those three categories. Some moments can be created, but many simply occur. Good leaders help the people they are mentoring to learn from them and make the most of them by explaining the experience and asking the right questions. All of us experience far more than we understand. Your job as a Level 5 leader is to help the high-level people you are developing to make sense out of what they experience and find value in it.

3. Use Your Own Crucible Moments as Guidelines to Teach Leaders

Every leader needs to draw upon his or her own crucible experiences and breakthroughs as material to help the next generation of leaders lead. To do that, you must have examined those experiences and identified the lessons you've learned from them. It's very likely that the experiences and lessons that allowed you to break through the leadership lids in your life will help others break through theirs.

My recommendation is that you set aside time with pen and paper (or computer) to identify your own crucible moments. Figure out how they might be able to help the people you're developing. Then tell your breakthrough experiences as stories to the leaders you desire to develop.

I have to warn you: some people will call you arrogant or egocentric when you tell them. Don't let that deter you. I know of no better way to communicate important truths to others. People have been using stories to teach life's lessons for as long as human beings have been walking the earth. Tell yours and help the next generation to take its place as leaders.

4. Expose Leaders to Other People and Organizations That Will Impact Them

One of the best ways I found to instill leadership qualities and skills into my developing leaders is to ask them to interview good leaders. Asking questions and looking for ways to develop a certain quality is a wonderful way for a person to grow. First, your developing leaders have to keep their eyes open for good leaders and well-led organizations, which begins to develop a leadership awareness in them. Second, they have to take the initiative (and sometimes be persuasive) to get the interview. Third, they have to prepare for the interview, which causes them to go deeper in their thinking about leadership. Fourth, the experience of the interview itself puts them in another leader's world and exposes them to another culture, which helps them to grow. And finally, analyzing the interview and talking about it with the person who gave them the assignment helps to make the lessons concrete—especially if they are required to implement and teach what they've learned. Many a time after I asked my developing leaders to do an interview, they came back and said, "I thought that this leadership quality was strong in my life until I witnessed it in another leader's life. I've got a long way to go."

Leaders on Level 5 have access to leadership, organizations, opportunities, and experiences that your emerging leaders don't. Make the most of them for their benefit. Even if you are not yet on the Pinnacle level, you still have access that your leaders don't. Share it. You can give your leaders experiences that will impact them for the rest of their lives and that may continue to create leadership ripples in future generations. Don't squander that opportunity.

Every time you develop a leader, you make a difference in the world. And if you develop leaders who take what they've learned and use it to develop other leaders, there's no telling what kind of an impact you'll have or how long that impact will last.

Conclusion

The leadership journey has the potential to take individuals through a lifelong process in three phases: learn, earn, return. People at the start of the journey who are given a position of leadership are faced with a decision. Are they going to learn now to lead better, or are they going to rely on their position, guard their turf, and play king of the hill to maintain what they've got? Those who choose to learn enter the learning phase and start to slowly climb up the levels of leadership. Typically, when they reach the Production level, they begin to receive recognition and the rewards of leadership. That's when most leaders enter the earning phase. Many are content to stay there. They climb the ladder in the organization, they have the respect of their peers, and they earn a good living. Only those leaders who decide to give back to others and develop other leaders enter the returning phase. Leaders who dedicate themselves to developing more leaders and pour themselves into the task, giving their best energies and resources to raise up other leaders, are the only ones who have the chance to move up to the Pinnacle.

No matter where you are in your own leadership journey, I encourage you to learn all you can and keep learning. And when you reach the earning phase, don't stop there. Don't lead others solely for your own benefit. Start giving to others and teaching them to lead so that you can enter the returning phase. Do that long enough and well enough, and you give yourself an opportunity to reach Level 5 and experience and share all the benefits of all five levels of leadership.

CHANGE YOUR THINKING,
CHANGE YOUR LIFE

WITH JOHN C. MAXWELL'S
WALL STREET JOURNAL BESTSELLER

HOW SUCCESSFUL PEOPLE THINK

Good thinkers are always in demand. They solve problems, never lack ideas, and always have hope for a better future. In this compact read for today's fast-paced world, Maxwell reveals eleven types of successful thinking, and how you can maximize each to revolutionize your work and life.

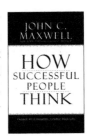

Also available from

[h] hachette **and** [h] hachette
AUDIO   DIGITAL

And look for the companion

HOW SUCCESSFUL PEOPLE THINK
WORKBOOK

Available now from
Center Street wherever books are sold.

CENTER
STREET

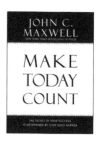

BET ON YOURSELF & REACH YOUR POTENTIAL

Growth is essential to your satisfaction and your success, but it doesn't just happen. It requires intentionality, focus and accountability. It also requires a plan. *The Maxwell Plan for Personal Growth* is designed for your busy lifestyle. It features twelve key areas for your growth and development:

PRINCIPLES OF GROWTH • ATTITUDE • CHARACTER • RELATIONSHIPS • GOALS • PRIORITIES • TEAMWORK • COMMUNICATION • INITIATIVE • THINKING • LEADERSHIP • MENTORING

Scan here to learn more or visit **www.MaxwellPlan.com**.

The JOHN MAXWELL **Co.**

www.johnmaxwell.com